ARE YOU A
Miserable
Old Bastard?

ARE YOU A
Miserable
Old Bastard?

Andrew John
and Stephen Blake

The Lyons Press
Guilford, Connecticut
An Imprint of The Globe Pequot Press

For Mickey,

at times a supremely grouchy bastard,
and thus a great inspiration.

Contents

* * *

Acknowledgments

Who reads acknowledgments pages? Nobody we know. Have you ever seen a well-thumbed acknowledgments page? Thought not. So why bother? Oh, we might just mention our dear editor, Helen Cumberbatch, who has grumbled and griped at us to get our text in on time. No doubt she's gone through it with her accustomed high proficiency and meticulous scrutiny, so, if there are any problems or inaccuracies, you can blame her.

Introduction

We know what you're thinking: Why write a book about being a miserable old bastard? Aren't there enough world-weary people around without encouraging more to crawl out of the woodwork? Well, if that is a genuine grouse on your part, join the club. You've just committed the ultimate grump: you've grumped about grumps. Congratulations! What do you want, a medal?

Are You a Miserable Old Bastard? takes a begrudging look at the world of the grouch, halfheartedly highlighting the many different sources of annoyance that are guaranteed to get the goat of moody moaners of all ages. Writing about miserable old bastards tends to bring out the grumpiness in you, which is just as well for us as writers because it's enabled us to grumble about pet subjects of our own: kids, animals, entertainment, media, politicians, technology—all the usual suspects. We've also included quotes and insights from a range of celebrated individuals: from art and literature—Ogden Nash, Oscar Wilde, Bertolt Brecht, Mark Twain, Charles Baudelaire, Samuel Beckett, Dorothy Parker; from politics—Lyndon B. Johnson, Winston Churchill, Benjamin Disraeli; from the world of film—Woody Allen, Groucho Marx, W. C. Fields, to name but a few.

These wonderful people have, over the years, redressed the balance and stopped cheery, airheaded, happy-clappy, optimistic halfwits from having it all their own way and making us think this wretched world is any better than it is. They have stood up, flown the flag, let themselves be counted, and used their art for the sake of grumpiness and malcontentedness—and long may their works live on.

Essentially, this unashamed miseryfest of a book amply provides you with all kinds of things to be grumpy about, as well as giving insights into the psyche of a miserable old bastard. If you're a bona fide grump, you'll agree with every word we say (although it'll be obvious that *some* of it is written with tongues firmly in cheeks and should be taken in the appropriate spirit).

So, as you can see, we've done our best in truly trying circumstances. We did tell our publishers we wouldn't actually *enjoy* putting together this cheerless, dismal little volume, that it would be far better if we just went into a corner and griped about how appalling things are—or just quietly withered away. They didn't respond.

And we were right. It's been a depressing slog from beginning to end and, quite frankly, you're welcome to it! In fact, we hope it makes you thoroughly cat-kickingly cantankerous, not to mention peevish, petulant, and downright irritable. *We're* off to the corner bar to complain about the beer and solve all the world's problems with all the other miserable old bastards.

* * *

Don't Talk to Me About Life,
or
Why We Get Miserable and Moody about Things in General

Life always comes to a bad end.
—Marcel Aymé, writer

Admit it: You love to moan, you savor the daily gripe, you look forward to a good old grouse. Let's face it, everybody's at it these days because there's so much to be miserable about! It's become the norm. How can we be happy about *anything* in this mad, mad world of ours?

For our part, we find plenty of things to be miserable about:

- technology that's supposed to make your life easier and save you time, and does neither

- politicians who want to collect all our personal details and sell them to megabucks corporations so they can target us in their marketing campaigns and try to sell us things no one with even the sanity of a brain-damaged wombat would want to buy—and all for the purpose of foisting unwanted ID cards on us

- the most powerful man on Planet Earth with his finger hovering over the nuclear button, who famously (or infamously) thinks that the French don't have a word for "entrepreneur" and once made an astonishing inquiry about which "state" Wales was in

- the way the national health service loses too many of its patients to virulent hospital bugs

- bleating religionists of the *really serious* variety who go whining to the newspapers if someone so much as *suggests* that their chosen faith, sect, or-cult might be just a tad intolerant

- millions of channels of total garbage on television

- trains that don't arrive on time—if they run at all

- millions *more* channels of total garbage on television

- bad grammar on the f****** TV—right where it *shouldn't* be . . .

And there's more. There's much more. The transport system is up a creek, with congested roads, overcrowded planes and subways; the nation's health is getting worse; standards in education are falling; and even the weather isn't what it used to be anymore.

But don't get us started! We could go on forever about life and the miseries it holds in store. Thankfully, several people—and a fictional robot—have at times felt downright grouchy enough to do it for us, and, in the interests of spreading a bit of crabbiness around, we bring you some of their grouchier moments . . .

QUOTABLE QUERULOUS QUIBBLES ABOUT LIFE

He who laughs has not yet heard the bad news.

BERTOLT BRECHT, POET AND PLAYWRIGHT

✳

Broadly speaking, human beings may be divided into three classes: those who are billed to death, those who are worried to death and those who are bored to death.

WINSTON CHURCHILL, BRITISH PRIME MINISTER

✳

For every complex problem, there is a solution that is simple, neat and wrong.

H. L. MENCKEN, JOURNALIST, CRITIC, AND EDITOR

✳

I know of no existing nation that deserves to live. And I know of very few individuals.

H. L. MENCKEN

✳ ✳ ✳

The older I get the more I admire and crave competence, just simple competence, in any field from adultery to zoology.
—H. L. MENCKEN

✳ ✳ ✳

What good is a long life to us if it is hard, joyless and so full of suffering that we can only welcome death as a deliverer?

SIGMUND FREUD, PHYSICIAN AND FOUNDER OF PSYCHOANALYSIS

"It's snowing still," said Eeyore gloomily.

"So it is."

"And freezing."

"Is it?"

"Yes," said Eeyore. *"However,"* he said, brightening up a little, *"we haven't had an earthquake recently."*

A. A. MILNE, AUTHOR (FROM *Winnie the Pooh*)

✻

"Good morning, Little Piglet," said Eeyore. *"If it is a good morning,"* he said. *"Which I doubt,"* said he. *"Not that it matters,"* he said.

A. A. MILNE (FROM *Winnie the Pooh*)

✻

Life? Don't talk to me about life.

Life, loathe it or ignore it, you can't like it.

Do you want me to sit in a corner and rust or just fall apart where I'm standing?

Don't pretend you want to talk to me, I know you hate me.

I only have to talk to somebody and they begin to hate me. Even robots hate me. If you just ignore me I expect I shall probably go away.

Here I am, brain the size of a planet, and they ask me to take you to the bridge. Call that job satisfaction? I don't.

Sorry, did I say something wrong? Pardon me for breathing, which I never do anyway so I don't know why I bother to say it; oh, God, I'm so depressed.

Don't feel you have to take any notice of me, please.

MARVIN THE PARANOID ANDROID, IN DOUGLAS ADAMS'S *The Hitchhiker's Guide to the Galaxy* AND ITS SEQUELS

Starbucks makes pretty good coffee. That's got to be a good thing. But it's all those newspapers and "Hey, wow" sofas, and the pain au raisin *that goes with it that I can't stand.*

BOB GELDOF, ROCK MUSICIAN,
AND LIVE AID AND LIVE 8 ORGANIZER

✳

My band calls me Victor Meldrew. My kids call me Victor Meldrew. I actually think that when my hair finally falls out I'll find that I probably am Victor Meldrew.

RICK WAKEMAN, MUSICIAN (VICTOR MELDREW WAS THE
GRUMPY MAIN CHARACTER PLAYED BY RICHARD WILSON
IN THE BRITISH TV SITCOM *One Foot in the Grave*)

✳

Of course it's possible to love a human being if you don't know them too well.

CHARLES BUKOWSKI, POET AND AUTHOR

To the discontented man no chair is easy.
—BENJAMIN FRANKLIN, AUTHOR, DIPLOMAT,
PHILOSOPHER, AND SCIENTIST

✳ ✳ ✳

At the ominous word "liberality," Scrooge frowned and shook his head.
CHARLES DICKENS, NOVELIST
(FROM *A Christmas Carol*)

∗ ∗ ∗

If it's good, they'll stop making it.
—HERBERT BLOCK, POLITICAL CARTOONIST

∗ ∗ ∗

Idealism is fine, but as it approaches reality the cost becomes prohibitive.
WILLIAM F. BUCKLEY JR.,
AUTHOR AND COMMENTATOR

∗

I just dress in what is comfortable and covers up my gut as much as possible, because the problem is that I look like a cab driver. You know, there are some of us that are just fated to look like a cab driver. It doesn't matter what clothes you put on, or how much you pay for them, you're still going to look like a cab driver.
JOHN PEEL, RADIO PERSONALITY AND DJ

∗ ∗ ∗

The world is so dreadfully managed, one hardly knows to whom to complain.
—RONALD FIRBANK, WRITER

∗ ∗ ∗

Those who have some means think that the most important thing in the world is love. The poor know that it is money.

GERALD BRENAN, ESSAYIST

✳

A conference is a gathering of important people who singly can do nothing, but together can decide that nothing can be done.

FRED ALLEN, COMEDIAN

✳

WINSTON CHURCHILL, *visiting Niagara Falls for the second time, was asked to his obvious irritation whether the falls looked the same as when, decades earlier, he had first seen them. "Well," he growled, "the principle seems the same. The water keeps falling over."*

✳

I have neither the scholar's melancholy, which is emulation; nor the musician's, which is fantastical; nor the courtier's, which is proud; nor the soldier's, which is ambitious; nor the lawyer's, which is politic; nor the lady's, which is nice; nor the lover's, which is all these: but it is a melancholy of mine own, compounded of many simples, extracted from many objects, and indeed the sundry contemplation of my travels, in which my often rumination wraps me in a most humorous sadness.

WILLIAM SHAKESPEARE, PLAYWRIGHT
(SPOKEN BY JACQUES IN *As You Like It*, ACT 4, SCENE I)

✳ ✳ ✳

Past and to come seems best; things present worst.

—WILLIAM SHAKESPEARE (SPOKEN BY THE ARCHBISHOP
IN *King Henry the Fourth, Part 2*, ACT 1, SCENE 3)

I don't want to achieve immortality through my work;
I want to achieve it through not dying.

WOODY ALLEN, FILM DIRECTOR AND SCREENWRITER

✳

More than any other time in history, mankind faces a crossroads. One
path leads to despair and utter hopelessness, the other to total extinc-
tion. Let us pray we have the wisdom to choose correctly.

WOODY ALLEN (IN *Side Effects*)

✳

It seemed the world was divided into good and bad people. The good
ones slept better . . . while the bad ones seemed to enjoy the waking
hours much more.

WOODY ALLEN (IN *Side Effects*)

✳ ✳ ✳

Life is divided into the horrible and the miserable.
—WOODY ALLEN (IN *Annie Hall*)

✳ ✳ ✳

Life is a concentration camp. You're stuck here and there's no way out,
and you can only rage impotently against your persecutors.

WOODY ALLEN

✳

It's not that I'm afraid to die. I just don't want to be there when it
happens.

WOODY ALLEN

Remember that as a teenager you are in the last stage of your life when you will be happy to hear that the phone is for you.

—Fran Lebowitz, journalist

* * *

People (a group that in my opinion has always attracted an undue amount of attention) have often been likened to snowflakes. This analogy is meant to suggest that each is unique—no two alike. This is quite patently not the case. People . . . are quite simply a dime a dozen. And, I hasten to add, their only similarity to snowflakes resides in their invariable and lamentable tendency to turn, after a few warm days, to slush.

Fran Lebowitz

*

They f**k you up, your mom and dad . . .

Philip Larkin, poet (from "This Be the Verse")

*

Ha! Easy for nuns to talk about giving up things. That's what they do for a living.

Garrison Keillor, writer and broadcaster

*

Experience is a good teacher, but she sends in terrific bills.

Minna Antrim, writer

* * *

Modern Life Is Rubbish
—Album and song title by the rock band Blur

Good morning—stupid.
—LUDWIG VAN BEETHOVEN, COMPOSER
(GREETING AN ASSISTANT)

✳ ✳ ✳

The G in AGA syndrome stands for Grumpiness, midway between the A for Anger that you feel when you are young, and the A for Acquiescence you feel when you realize it's all gone to hell and there is nothing you can do about it.
STUART PREBBLE, EXECUTIVE PRODUCER AND WRITER OF THE BBC
SERIES *Grumpy Old Men*

✳

The average man's opinions are much less foolish than they would be if he thought for himself.
BERTRAND RUSSELL, PHILOSOPHER AND MATHEMATICIAN

A market is a place set apart for men to deceive and get the better of one another.

ANACHARSIS, GREEK PHILOSOPHER, SIXTH CENTURY BCE

* * *

If you want to annoy your neighbors, tell the truth about them.
—PIETRO ARETINO, SATIRIST

* * *

What passes for optimism is most often the effect of an intellectual error.

RAYMOND ARON, POLITICAL THINKER

*

People seem to enjoy things more when they know a lot of other people have been left out on the pleasure.

RUSSELL BAKER, HUMORIST

* * *

Inanimate objects are classified scientifically into three major categories—those that don't work, those that break down, and those that get lost.
—RUSSELL BAKER

* * *

I don't know what is worse: old men moaning, or people moaning about old men moaning, or people moaning about moaners moaning about moaning. . . . Modern life is full of opportunities, make the most of it!

DAN, CONTRIBUTOR TO A BBC WEB SITE

Nothing matters very much,
and few things matter at all.
—ARTHUR JAMES BALFOUR, BRITISH PRIME MINISTER
(ATTRIBUTED)

✳ ✳ ✳

If you would know what the Lord God thinks of money, you have only to look at those to whom he gives it.

MAURICE BARING, NOVELIST AND CRITIC

✳

What we call "progress" is the exchange of one nuisance for another nuisance.

HAVELOCK ELLIS, SEXOLOGIST

A great many people think they are thinking when they are merely rearranging their prejudices.

WILLIAM JAMES, PHILOSOPHER

✳

Life is a hospital in which every patient is possessed by the desire to change his bed.

CHARLES BAUDELAIRE, POET

✳ ✳ ✳

The reason we drive cars is that, once we've got one, we're free. But the conflict between that idealism and the reality that you get in your car is that you're exposed not to freedom, opportunities, discovery, delight—you're exposed to frustration, dirt, danger, and aggression, and that's what makes us so cross. That, I believe, is the source of road rage.

—STEPHEN BAYLEY, WRITER, CRITIC, AND STYLE GURU

✳ ✳ ✳

*I've had hypnotherapy, acupuncture, people hitting me with twigs. I had another man who electrocuted me every time I had a fag. That didn't stop me. Oh, dear, it's a terrible thing. Grumpy old man? This is my sixth day without a cigarette and I could rip your f***ing head off.*

ARTHUR SMITH, WRITER AND COMEDIAN

Why did nature create Man? Was it to show that she is big enough to make mistakes, or was it pure ignorance?
                    HOLBROOK JACKSON, JOURNALIST AND WRITER

✳ ✳ ✳

One has to look out for engineers—they begin with sewing machines and end up with the atomic bomb.
—MARCEL PAGNOL, PLAYWRIGHT

✳ ✳ ✳

Rantings of a
Miserable Old Bastard:
Part I

T here are some things you read in newspapers, hear on the radio, or watch on TV that have obviously been deliberately chosen to stimulate the crabby and cantankerous components of your autonomic nervous system; items that have been put there just to get people going. Here's a selection of the kind of stuff that makes you want to screw up the paper you read them in and throw it at the radio or TV that you heard them on.

- George W. Bush once asked the Welsh singer Charlotte Church which state Wales was in. (In a better state than America, no doubt.)

- The antidepressant drug with the generic name of paroxetine was raising concern in August 2005 because, according to scientists in Oslo, far from relieving depression it was causing people to become suicidal. Well, opting to do yourself in is definitely one way to cure your depression.

- You have a problem with your line and call the phone company. Their maddening, merry-go-round menu system has you jabbing at keys till your fingertips bleed, and you eventually find yourself trying to explain the problem to a nerdy sixteen-year-old "adviser" whose communications skills are only marginally superior to those of an adolescent chimp. After it becomes painfully obvious that you'd be better off climbing up the telephone pole and fixing the problem yourself, your rage has become so extreme it could power the national grid. Eventually the phone employee gives you a number to call, and when you put the phone down to dial the number that was grunted at you, it's only when you're halfway through the menu system that you realize it's the same number you dialed forty-five minutes ago. After dunking your head in a bowl of icy water and knocking back several stiff drinks, you contact a cable company or a satellite phone service and cancel your account with the phone company. That'll show the bastards.

White Heat and Snake Oil,
or
Why Technology Is
So Often a Load of Crap

*The thing with high-tech is that you
always end up using scissors.*
—DAVID HOCKNEY, ARTIST

Do people for one minute think that all those labor-saving gizmos that are supposed to give us all the freedom in the world actually work? Hardly. In fact, we're all working harder than ever. What we did end up with, though, was a host of utterly useless creations that do more to antagonize us than to help us cope with the daily grind:

- cell phones with infuriating ringtones that sound like frogs on crack

- the opportunity to speak to a call center agent in Bombay to find out the size of our unauthorized overdraft at our bank, whose local branch was just down the road till it was transferred to the other end of the country and merged with a sock manufacturer

- instruction booklets written in Klingon by Martians who failed their high school course in intergalactic languages

- silicon snake oil in the form of gadgets you never knew you wanted until you were told you couldn't do without them

We've now got more TV channels than you can shake a digital box at, all offering total crap, thereby proving that choice and quality are inversely proportional to each other. We have cell phones with cameras that have enabled juvenile thugs to go around filming attacks on total strangers and sending the images to their equally reprobate friends.

Doesn't it make you grumpy *when . . .*

. . . you've been slaving over a hot computer for an hour, but you forget to save or back up your files so that when the system suddenly crashes, you end up losing all your precious work? Though it may be possible to retrieve the lost data with the help of experts, you know it'll be quicker (and a lot cheaper) to begin from scratch, even though the mere thought of it makes you break out in a cold sweat.

We all know what it's like when an item of apparently advanced technology fails to deliver the goods, when it suddenly stops doing what it's supposed to be doing, when batteries fail after only a few uses, when cell phones stop accepting calls, digital cameras stop taking pictures, and DVD players stop playing DVDs. Worst of all is when you're trying to figure out why something won't work and you have to wade through a three-inch-thick manual printed on third-rate toilet paper in pidgin English. After ten minutes it's obvious you're getting nowhere fast, and you'd probably be better off reading it in French.

Vorsprung durch Technik (German for "progress through technology")? Get real!

Such a despairing attitude among users of "modern" technology is far from unique in this day and age, as quite a few other people are less than blissful about the so-called technological revolution, too . . .

Quotable Querulous Quibbles about Technology

The biggest lie that the technology manufacturers sell you is, "Plug and go." It's "Plug and f**k me, I don't know what's going on here," and it's hours and hours.

"What are you doing in there?" from the kitchen.

*"I've just bought a new gadget, darling, and I'm just sorting it out."
And it goes on for weeks, you know. "Plug and go"? It's a joke.*

Michael Grade, chairman of the BBC

To err is human, but to really foul things up requires a computer.

PHILIP HOWARD,
JOURNALIST AND AUTHOR

❊

Computers are anti-Faraday machines. He [Faraday] said he couldn't understand anything until he could count it, while computers count everything and understand nothing.

RALPH CORNES, *The Guardian*

✳ ✳ ✳

One machine can do the work of fifty ordinary men. No machine can do the work of one extraordinary man.

—ELBERT HUBBARD,
WRITER, PUBLISHER, AND EDITOR

✳ ✳ ✳

If you put tomfoolery into a computer, nothing comes out but tomfoolery. But this tomfoolery, having passed through a very expensive machine, is somehow ennobled and no one dares criticize it.

PIERRE GALLOIS, SCIENTIST

❊

Machines are worshipped because they are beautiful, and valued because they confer power; they are hated because they are hideous, and loathed because they impose slavery.

BERTRAND RUSSELL, PHILOSOPHER

Mechanics, not microbes, are the menace to civilization.

NORMAN DOUGLAS, WRITER

One servant is worth a thousand gadgets.
—JOSEPH ALOIS SCHUMPETER,
ECONOMIST AND SOCIAL THEORIST

✳ ✳ ✳

Technology . . . the knack of so arranging the world that we need not experience it.

MAX FRISCH, PLAYWRIGHT

✳

A modern computer hovers between the obsolescent and the nonexistent.

SYDNEY BRENNER, SCIENTIST

If the human race wants to go to hell in a basket, technology can help it get there by jet.

CHARLES M. ALLEN, SCIENTIST

❊

The unleashed power of the atom has changed everything save our modes of thinking and we thus drift toward unparalleled catastrophe.

ALBERT EINSTEIN, MATHEMATICIAN

✳ ✳ ✳

It has become appallingly obvious that our technology has exceeded our humanity.
—ALBERT EINSTEIN

✳ ✳ ✳

Science and technology multiply around us. To an increasing extent they dictate the languages in which we speak and think. Either we use those languages, or we remain mute.

J. G. BALLARD, WRITER

❊

Technology causes problems as well as solves problems. Nobody has figured out a way to ensure that, as of tomorrow, technology won't create problems. Technology simply means increased power, which is why we have the global problems we face today.

JARED DIAMOND, PHYSIOLOGIST

No crash-proof [computer] system can be built unless it is made for an idiot.
Ellen Ullman, writer

✳ ✳ ✳

As we push our technologies to exploit more and more resources, we now recognize that both the direct devastation and the unforeseen consequences are becoming increasingly global in nature.
—Richard Norgaard, writer

✳ ✳ ✳

The ethic of progress—in effect, the ethic of perpetual technospheric expansion—is in reality no more than an ethic of biospheric destruction . . . it is an anti-evolutionary ethic.
Edward Goldsmith, ecologist and business executive

Sirs, I have tested your machine. It adds a new terror to life and makes death a long-felt want.
—Herbert Beerbohm Tree, actor and theatrical impresario, referring to a gramophone (attributed)

✳ ✳ ✳

The telephone is a good way to talk to people without having to offer them a drink.

FRAN LEBOWITZ, JOURNALIST

✳

In these days of computer viruses, asking if you may put your disk into someone's computer is the technological equivalent of unsafe sex.
RUTH DUDLEY EDWARDS, HISTORIAN, WRITER, AND JOURNALIST

✳ ✳ ✳

I've heard that myth quite seriously expressed . . . that the beast in the Book of Revelation will be a monster computer.
—BILL ELLIS, SPECIALIST IN MODERN FOLKLORE

✳ ✳ ✳

The Science of Being a Grump,
or
Why It's Perfectly Normal to Be a Miserable Old Bastard

*Oh, wouldn't the world seem dull and flat
With nothing whatever to grumble at?*
—W. S. GILBERT, PLAYWRIGHT AND LIBRETTIST

Believe it or not, scientists at Vanderbilt University in Nashville, Tennessee, discovered that some people are naturally predisposed to having a grumpy outlook on life simply because they're born that way—it's in their genes.

In 2002, psychologist David Zald identified a small area of the brain that he believes controls people's tendency to frequent attacks of anger, irritability, or anxiety. The more active that section of the brain, the more likely a person will suffer from bad moods and general grumpiness.

According to Zald: "It looks like it is this part of the brain's activity that regulates people's mood. It is also a part of the brain that controls sweating, stomach acidity and heart rate, and other physical feelings associated with stress and bad moods."

This particular part of the human brain, which is no bigger than a postage stamp, is called the ventromedial prefrontal cortex; it lies an inch or two behind the right eye. Zald used eighty-nine people in his study, and scanned their brains using a technique known as positron emission tomography, or PET. These men and women were then asked to complete a detailed survey of their state of mind over the last month. Those who experienced many bad moods were also revealed to have a lot of extra activity in the ventromedial prefrontal cortex.

Zald's research is backed up by studies on people who have suffered damage in that area of the brain, who often lose the ability to feel angst or stress. "They could literally think to themselves: 'Should I bet that $10,000 on a roll of the dice?' and not feel anything in the pit of their stomach. They just don't feel anxiety, which is linked to bad moods," said Zald.

So there you have it—the perfect excuse to justify being a miserable old bastard!

**Signs to look for if you think you might have
turned into a miserable old bastard:**

- when you get home from work or from a shopping spree you've got at least three gripes to share with your partner or family

- you whine at every opportunity

- tuts and heavy sighs punctuate your conversations with disturbing frequency

- you generally see the worst in every situation

- any moments of happiness you experience are few and short-lived

- you realize you haven't smiled or laughed in weeks

All Creatures Great and Vile,
or
Why Do Animals Annoy the Hell Out of You?

God in his wisdom made the fly
And then forgot to tell us why.
—OGDEN NASH, POET AND HUMORIST

What is it that gives all dogs, no matter what their breed, the right to sniff at one's crotch? And why do they always do it in front of an audience?

Is it simply to maximize embarrassment, perhaps?

It's always the same: you're trying to be polite during a chance encounter with a dog-owning neighbor, and before you can take evasive action, the bothersome beast is coming at you at ninety miles an hour before burying his nose in your groin, and sniffing and grunting loudly. In spite of your obvious discomfort, rather than drag the annoying mutt away from you, the neighbor invariably gazes fondly at her dear little bundle of fur, remarking on his playful nature and assuring you that he is "just being friendly." Occasionally, when your plight has been ignored for too long, it becomes necessary to take matters into your own hands: deploying a subtle little kick (in the direction of the beast, not its owner) can often be used to good effect. "Funny," you say  above the high-pitched yelping, "something seems to have spooked the little fella."

Dogs also have fleas—nasty, germ-carrying creatures that any self-respecting creator should have thought twice about inflicting upon the earth. With about 1,600 species of fleas in existence across the globe, the world's entire flea population probably weighs more than the world's humans. If your dog has fleas, although there may be only a couple of dozen on the creature, there will be another 10,000 on the carpet waiting to jump on your warm-blooded body to hitch a ride elsewhere.

Cats carry fleas, too. While a dog will at least pretend to be your friend, a cat has an icy contempt for anything but itself, and you know damned well that the only reason it stays with you is because you give it food. If it jumps into your lap it's simply because it

 senses that you're more comfortable than the floor. It hates you. You're just a convenient bed with a bolted-on feeding facility.

And when it brings a pathetic little bunch of blood and feathers that was once a living, vibrant, melodious little bird, *and gives it to you as a present*, it's disgusting.

> # Doesn't it make you grumpy *when* . . .
>
> . . . you're doing some weeding in the garden and you stumble across a pile of "doings" undoubtedly left by next-door's tabby? Doesn't it sometimes make you feel like climbing into next-door's garden in the dead of night and leaving your own calling card, to see how your neighbor likes it?

And what about those furry little things like gerbils, guinea pigs, rabbits, and hamsters? What do you *do* with a hamster, for goodness' sake?

Many people seem to have a pet mentality combined with an anthropomorphic view of pets: "Oh, they're so cute and wouldn't hurt a fly [they'd be more useful if they did] and ever so intelligent, you know." Yeah, they're clever enough to know that the disgusting brown mush you've just spooned out of the can is food, and that if they pretend to show you unconditional love and affection they'll be fed and taken care of until their dying day.

We're obviously not alone in maintaining a healthy distrust of these four-legged fiends, as this selection of opinions clearly shows.

QUOTABLE QUERULOUS QUIBBLES ABOUT CREATURES

People who hate children and small dogs can't be all bad.

W. C. FIELDS, ACTOR AND COMEDIAN

✳

The rabbit has a charming face;
Its private life is a disgrace.
I really dare not name to you
The awful things that rabbits do . . .

ANONYMOUS (1925)

To my mind, the only possible pet is a cow.
Cows love you. . . . They will listen to your
problems and never ask a thing in return.
They will be your friends forever.
And, when you get tired of them, you
can kill and eat them. Perfect.
—BILL BRYSON, WRITER

✳ ✳ ✳

*The trouble with a kitten is that
When it grows up it's always a cat.*

OGDEN NASH, POET AND HUMORIST

✳

*Cats are bastards . . . If cats could find a way to push all the people in
the world into an active volcano and still open all the tins of cat food,
they would . . . Cats are, in short, the scum of the earth.*

DAVID QUANTICK, COMEDIAN AND WRITER

✳

*And as for those old women who have nothing better to do than go out
and spread the contents of their bread bins all over your local green
space so that pigeons will come along and empty their bowels over
everything and everyone—wouldn't you just love to see one of those
old dears feeding the pigeons one sunny morning and suddenly an
unmarked van screech up, the doors fly open and four masked men
leap out, throw her in the back, and she's never seen again?*

DAVID QUANTICK

There are more ways of killing a cat than
choking her with cream.

—CHARLES KINGSLEY, NOVELIST AND CLERIC

✳ ✳ ✳

Cats seem to go on the principle that it never does any harm to ask for what you want.

JOSEPH WOOD KRUTCH, ESSAYIST AND NATURALIST

✻

Laboratory guinea pigs say to themselves: "I bet they would not do that to polar bears."

RAMÓN GÓMEZ DE LA SERNA, NOVELIST

The old gray donkey, Eeyore, stood by himself in a thistly corner of the Forest, his front feet well apart, his head on one side, and thought about things. Sometimes he thought sadly to himself, "Why?" and sometimes he thought, "Wherefore?" and sometimes he thought, "Inasmuch as which?" and sometimes he didn't quite know what he was thinking about.

—A. A. MILNE, AUTHOR
(FROM *Winnie the Pooh*)

✳ ✳ ✳

You know, I have never deliberately run over a fox. They are always too quick for me. But dogs. I don't like dogs. Because owners always assume you like their dogs as much as they do.

RORY MCGRATH, COMEDIAN

✳ ✳ ✳

Cats are autocrats of naked self-interest.
They are both amoral and immoral,
consciously breaking rules. . . . the cat
may be the only animal who savors the
perverse or reflects upon it.
—CAMILLE PAGLIA, ACADEMIC AND AUTHOR

✳ ✳ ✳

Songs for the Sad,
Music for the Miserable

"Heaven Knows I'm Miserable Now"—The Smiths

"Why Does It Always Rain on Me?"—Travis

"Prayers for Rain"—The Cure

"I Hate Myself and Want To Die"—Nirvana

"Without You"—Mariah Carey

"Girlfriend in a Coma"—The Smiths

"Happy Being Miserable"—Leningrad Cowboys

"Ain't No Sunshine"—Bill Withers

"Misery"—Soul Asylum

"I Don't Like Mondays"—The Boomtown Rats

"Rainy Days and Mondays (Always Get Me Down)"—The Carpenters

"Mardy Bum"—Arctic Monkeys

"(I) Love to Hate You"—Erasure

The Medium Is the Massage,
or
Why We Are Not Amused by TV and
Other Attempts to Divert and Inform Us

In California they don't throw their garbage away—
they make it into television shows.

—WOODY ALLEN, FILM DIRECTOR AND SCREENWRITER

TV today is undoubtedly a shadow of its former self, particularly now that there is barely anything on the small screen of any real value. Take reality TV shows, such as *Big Brother*, as a case in point. A bunch of fame-hungry losers are put in a specially constructed house and told to act "normal." For weeks on end the viewing public watches these pathetic wretches uttering the most boring and inane crap, and, while the most annoying people get evicted, others stay in. The winner becomes an instant celebrity . . . for about fifteen nanoseconds, and then they're forgotten because *Slightly Well-Known People Watch Paint Dry While Playing with Their Private Parts* has just begun on another channel.

Then there are those programs whose sole aim is to make you throw up into your TV dinner. There was *Nip and Tuck*, a reality show that gleefully encouraged you to witness flabby, spoiled, loaded dolts having bits removed, sewn up, pulled a bit this way and a bit that way, stretched, loosened, and sucked out. Yuck! This is not to be confused with the similarly titled *Nip/Tuck*, a drama series that gleefully encouraged you to witness flabby, spoiled, wealthy dolts having bits removed, sewn up, pulled a bit this way and a bit that way, stretched, loosened, and sucked out.

Doesn't it make you grumpy *when* . . .

. . . you're watching TV at dinnertime, when, in the middle of a series of commercials, you're confronted with a cream to cure hemorrhoids, or an ad about tampons, yeast infections, or incontinence pads? Surely such ads could be confined to time slots when viewers are less likely to be in the middle of their lunchtime snack or evening meal.

"Sixteen channels of shit," sang Pink Floyd on the band's album *The Wall*. How right they were. . . . You can get digital boxes now, or one of those weird-shaped satellite dishes that decorate virtually every house in the known universe, which bring not sixteen but sixty channels of it. And then some.

Then there are twenty-four-hour news channels that have so much information plastered all over the screen you can't possibly take it all in at once. And half the screen is always covered with vast areas of garish color that do nothing more than obscure vital bits of the pictures of the current news story with scrolling text. It's pure information overload. And what about the annoying little icons in the bottom corners of the screen that tell you you're tuned to ABC or HGTV? Surely viewers know which channel they're watching because they chose it in the first place . . . Give the viewing public *some* credit, please!

Grumps of page and screen

Before we leave entertainment, writers, and media in general, we ought to pay honorable tribute to a few notable grumps who have brought a little reassuringly depressing gloom and despondency to our lives.

W. C. Fields

Much quoted in these pages—because we think his acerbic wit is so funny and often so close to the truth—is W. C. Fields (1880–1946), born William Claude Dukenfield in Philadelphia, Pennsylvania.

This stocky, bulbous-nosed, leathery-faced figure with the gravelly voice was a juggler at the start of his professional life, and did the vaudeville circuits throughout the United States, South Africa, and Europe. Fields starred in several silent films, and his fans were well aware that he was a curmudgeon off screen as well as on.

Dorothy Parker

Another favorite wit is Dorothy Parker (1893–1967), famed for that razor-sharp *mot juste*. She was born in New Jersey, and was a drama critic for *Vanity Fair* and *Vogue*. She wrote reviews, short stories, and sketches—and of course poems—all vehicles for her sardonic humor.

Ambrose Bierce

Compiler of that wonderful work *The Devil's Dictionary* (1911), Ambrose Bierce (1842–c.1914) is another favorite of ours.

Bierce sharpened his political wit by becoming a political journalist. After the Civil War, he wrote satirical political pieces for the *San Francisco News Letter,* which he eventually edited. After moving to London, England, he began writing caustic material for *Figaro* and *Fun* magazines under the name of Dod Grile. A fascination with death and horror earned him the nickname "Bitter" Bierce.

Groucho Marx

And finally, the talented comedian whose first name says grouchiness itself, Groucho Marx (1895–1977). In the legendary films he made with his brothers Chico, Harpo, and Zeppo, Groucho's immediately identifiable character was that of a man with a huge cigar, a big moustache, and a sizable wit to match. After his film career, he continued in entertainment as master of ceremonies of a television series, *You Bet Your Life,* and wrote the autobiographical *Groucho and Me* (1959) and *Memoirs of a Mangy Lover* (1964).

Many of the quotable quotes from this caustic wit are arguably of the humorously grumpy variety:

"I was married by a judge. I should have asked for a jury."

"I worked myself up from nothing to a state of extreme poverty."

"No one is completely unhappy at the failure of his best friend."

"There is one way to find out if a man is honest—ask him. If he says 'Yes,' you know he is crooked."

"Why, I'd horse-whip you if I had a horse."

"You've got the brain of a four-year-old boy, and I'll bet he was glad to get rid of it."

"Now there's a man with an open mind—you can feel the breeze from here!"

Quotable Querulous Quibbles about Entertainment and the Media

A medium, so called because it is neither rare nor well done.

Ernie Kovacs, entertainer
(an attributed remark about television)

✳

I got tired of seeing television shows that consist of a car crash, a gunman, and a hooker talking to a black pimp. It was cheaper to do a new series than to throw out my family's television sets.

Bill Cosby, actor, author, and comedian

✳ ✳ ✳

I read the newspaper avidly. It is my one form of continuous fiction.
—Aneurin Bevan, politician

It is stupidvision—where most of the actors look like they have to pretend to be stupid because they think their audience is . . . It patronizes. It talks to the vacuum cleaner and the washing machine without much contact with the human brain.
—POLLY TOYNBEE, JOURNALIST
(SAID OF DAYTIME TELEVISION)

✳ ✳ ✳

The only "ism" Hollywood believes in is plagiarism.
DOROTHY PARKER, HUMORIST, CRITIC, AND WRITER

✳

This is not a book that should be tossed lightly aside. It should be hurled with great force.
DOROTHY PARKER
(REFERRING TO A NOVEL BY BENITO MUSSOLINI)

✳

She ran the whole gamut of the emotions from A to B.
DOROTHY PARKER (REFERRING TO
KATHARINE HEPBURN ON BROADWAY; ATTRIBUTED)

✳

"Media" is a word that has come to mean bad journalism.
GRAHAM GREENE, NOVELIST

Television? The word is half Greek and half Latin. No good can come of it.

C. P. SCOTT, JOURNALIST (ATTRIBUTED)

✳

TV is faster-paced generally these days—soaps are mainly responsible for that. The attention span has dropped so that few scenes these days last longer than two minutes.

I sound like a grumpy old man. Hell, I am!

GARY RUSSELL,
WRITER AND PRODUCER

✳

Chewing gum for the eyes.

FRANK LLOYD WRIGHT, ARCHITECT
(AN ATTRIBUTED REMARK MADE ABOUT TELEVISION)

✳ ✳ ✳

I've finally figured out why soap operas are, and logically should be, so popular with generations of housebound women. They are the only place in our culture where grown-up men take seriously all the things that grown-up women have to deal with all day long.

—GLORIA STEINEM, FEMINIST AND WRITER

✳ ✳ ✳

Lloyd Webber's music is everywhere, but so is AIDS.
SIR MALCOLM WILLIAMSON, COMPOSER
(SAID OF ANDREW LLOYD WEBBER'S MUSICAL *Sunset Boulevard*)

An American musical so bad that at times I longed for the boy-meets-tractor theme of Soviet drama.
—BERNARD LEVIN, JOURNALIST (SAID OF THE EMINENTLY FORGETTABLE 1961 RODGERS AND HAMMERSTEIN MUSICAL *Flower Drum Song*)

* * *

In old days men had the rack. Now they have the press.
OSCAR WILDE, PLAYWRIGHT AND POET

*

A magazine is simply a device to induce people to read advertising.
JAMES COLLINS, ADVERTISING EXECUTIVE

Advertising—a judicious mixture of flattery and threats.

NORTHROP FRYE, LITERARY CRITIC

✳

In the United States today, we have more than our share of the nattering nabobs of negativism. They have formed their own 4-H Club—the hopeless, hysterical hypochondriacs of history.

VICE PRESIDENT SPIRO T. AGNEW
(SAID OF THE PRESS IN 1970)

✳

A reporter is a man who has renounced everything in life but the world, the flesh, and the devil.

DAVID MURRAY, JOURNALIST AND WRITER

A great many people now reading and writing would be better employed keeping rabbits.
—EDITH SITWELL, AUTHOR

✳ ✳ ✳

Abstract art? A product of the untalented sold by the unprincipled to the utterly bewildered.

ALL CAPP, CARTOONIST

❋

An editor should have a pimp for a brother so he'd have someone to look up to.

GENE FOWLER, JOURNALIST

❋

I don't hate the press: I find a lot of it very unpalatable. But if that's the way they want to behave . . .

PRINCE PHILIP, DUKE OF EDINBURGH

❋

I'm sure they have a special screening where they go, "I'm sorry but you don't appear to be a nutter, so we can't actually put you on the air." Any debate about war or dictators will go straight to Hitler. Or any debate about technology will go straight to "Well, we've put a man on the moon." There's actually a rule in the BBC charter which says that only people talking in total clichés are allowed to be put in these programs.

JOHN O'FARRELL, WRITER

❋

Editor: a person employed by a newspaper whose business it is to separate the wheat from the chaff and to see that chaff is printed.

ELBERT HUBBARD, WRITER, PRINTER, AND EDITOR

Television was the ultimate evidence of cultural anemia.
—ROY A. K. HEATH, NOVELIST AND TEACHER

✳ ✳ ✳

The fact that a man is a newspaper reporter is evidence of some flaw of character.

PRESIDENT LYNDON B. JOHNSON

✶

It used to be that we in films were the lowest form of art. Now we have something to look down on.

BILLY WILDER, FILM DIRECTOR, WRITER, AND PRODUCER (SAID OF TELEVISION)

✶

From any cross-section of ads, the general advertiser's attitude would seem to be: if you are a lousy, smelly, idle, underprivileged, and over-sexed status-seeking neurotic moron, give me your money.

KENNETH BROMFIELD, ADVERTISING ILLUSTRATOR

✶

When distant and unfamiliar and complex things are communicated to great masses of people, the truth suffers a considerable and often a radical distortion. The complex is made over into the simple, the hypo-thetical into the dogmatic, and the relative into an absolute.

WALTER LIPPMANN, WRITER AND JOURNALIST

✶

The celebrity is a person who is known for his well-knownness.

DANIEL J. BOORSTIN, WRITER AND HISTORIAN

Perfume ads may not tell you anything about the products they're selling, but they do accurately describe the state of your mind if you drink some.

DAVID QUANTICK, COMEDIAN AND WRITER

✳

The near equivalent of actual conmen, loan-ad presenters are inches away from being criminals. They are saying, "I am famous so take my advice and get more into debt than you were before." Vile filth.

DAVID QUANTICK

✳

An author is a fool who, not content with having bored those who have lived with him, insists on boring future generations.

CHARLES DE SECONDAT, BARON DE MONTESQUIEU,
PHILOSOPHER, WRITER, AND LAWYER

✳ ✳ ✳

Hollywood is a place where they'll pay you
a thousand dollars for a kiss and
fifty cents for your soul.
—MARILYN MONROE, FILM ACTRESS

✳ ✳ ✳

A character actor is one who cannot act and therefore makes an elaborate study of disguise and stage tricks by which acting can be grotesquely simulated.

GEORGE BERNARD SHAW,
PLAYWRIGHT AND WRITER (ATTRIBUTED)

Acting is the most minor of gifts. After all, Shirley Temple could do it when she was four.

KATHARINE HEPBURN, FILM ACTRESS (ATTRIBUTED)

✳ ✳ ✳

Acting is therefore the lowest of the arts, if it is an art at all.
—GEORGE MOORE, WRITER

✳ ✳ ✳

Actors should be treated like cattle.

ALFRED HITCHCOCK, FILM DIRECTOR

✳

The media. It sounds like a convention of spiritualists.

TOM STOPPARD, PLAYWRIGHT AND SCREENWRITER

✳

All Stanislavsky ever said was, "Avoid generalities."

ANTHONY HOPKINS, ACTOR

✳

No! Not at any price. . . . When I am through with this picture I hope never to hear of Dracula again. I cannot stand it. . . . I do not intend that it shall possess me. No one knows what I suffer from the role.

BÉLA LUGOSI, FILM ACTOR
(HE'D BEEN ASKED TO PLAY THE ROLE ON STAGE,
AND GOT RATHER GRUMPY ABOUT IT.)

Oh, my God! Remember you're in Egypt. The skay *is only seen in Kensington.*

HERBERT BEERBOHM TREE, ACTOR AND THEATRICAL IMPRESARIO
(AN ACTRESS HAD TAKEN HER AFFECTED PRONUNCIATION
OF "SKY" TO EGYPT WITH HER; ATTRIBUTED)

✳

Well, I suppose the media are such a major industry now, and it needs feeding, so rather than wait for celebrity to happen they sort of invent it in order to report on it. Do you know what I mean? You don't necessarily have to wait any more. You just make it up as you go along.

BILL NIGHY, ACTOR

✳

Seventeen years of reputation doesn't really matter to a media that sniffs blood.

ANITA RODDICK, BUSINESS EXECUTIVE AND BODY SHOP FOUNDER
(SAID OF A FALL IN THE BODY SHOP'S FORTUNES)

✳ ✳ ✳

Advertising may be described as the science
of arresting human intelligence long
enough to get money from it.
—STEPHEN LEACOCK, HUMORIST AND ECONOMIST

✳ ✳ ✳

She looked as though butter wouldn't melt in her mouth—or anywhere else.

ELSA LANCHESTER, ACTRESS (REFERRING TO
MAUREEN O'HARA; ATTRIBUTED)

Advertising . . . legitimizes the idealized, stereotyped roles of women as temptress, wife, mother, and sex object.

LUCY KOMISAR, WRITER

✳

Don't Tell My Mother I Work in an Advertising Agency—She Thinks I Play Piano in a Whorehouse

JACQUES SÉGUÉLA, ADVERTISING EXECUTIVE
(TITLE OF A MEMOIR ABOUT BEING AN ADVERTISING EXECUTIVE)

✳ ✳ ✳

I think that I shall never see
A billboard lovely as a tree.
Perhaps unless the billboards fall,
I'll never see a tree at all.
—OGDEN NASH, POET AND HUMORIST

✳ ✳ ✳

I turned on the news and discovered that they took Tom McDonald's desk away. He's just standing there, and you think, "What's that all about?" And gradually it dawns on you that somebody must have said, "I've got an idea that will really make the news-viewing experience much improved—we'll take your desk away." How do they possibly see this sort of thing as an improvement?

BILL BRYSON, WRITER

✳

Some of the greatest love affairs I've known involved one actor—unassisted.

WILSON MIZNER, PLAYWRIGHT (ATTRIBUTED)

History will see advertising as one of the real evil things of our time. It is stimulating people constantly to want things, want this, want that.
MALCOLM MUGGERIDGE, JOURNALIST AND COMMENTATOR
(ATTRIBUTED)

∗

I have had my aerials removed—it's the moral equivalent of a prostate operation.

MALCOLM MUGGERIDGE

∗

I don't care for modern films. Cars crashing over cliffs and close-ups of people's feet.

LILLIAN GISH, ACTRESS

∗

The gift of broadcasting is, without question, the lowest human capacity to which any man could attain.
HAROLD NICOLSON, DIPLOMAT, WRITER, AND CRITIC

∗ ∗ ∗

Rock journalism is people who can't write interviewing people who can't talk for people who can't read.
—FRANK ZAPPA, COMPOSER AND ROCK MUSICIAN

∗ ∗ ∗

Any little pinhead who makes one picture is called a "star."
HUMPHREY BOGART, ACTOR (ATTRIBUTED)

I didn't like the play, but then I saw it under adverse conditions—the curtain was up.

—GROUCHO MARX, COMEDIAN

✳ ✳ ✳

Educational television should be absolutely forbidden. It can only lead to unreasonable disappointment when your child discovers that the letters of the alphabet do not leap up out of books and dance around with royal-blue chickens.

FRAN LEBOWITZ, JOURNALIST

✳

You can fool all of the people all of the time if the advertising is right and the budget is big enough.

JOSEPH E. LEVINE, FILM PRODUCER

✳

When a man throws an empty cigarette package from an automobile, he is liable to a fine of fifty dollars. When a man throws a billboard across a view, he is richly rewarded.

PAT BROWN, POLITICIAN

✳ ✳ ✳

If there's anything disgusting about the movie business, it's the whoredom of my peers.

—SEAN PENN, ACTOR AND FILM DIRECTOR

✳ ✳ ✳

Jazz: music invented for the torture of imbeciles.
—HENRY VAN DYKE, CLERGYMAN AND EDUCATOR

✱ ✱ ✱

He's the kind of guy that, when he dies, he gives God a bad time for making him bald.

MARLON BRANDO, ACTOR
(REFERRING TO FRANK SINATRA)

✳

An actor's a guy who, if you ain't talking about him, ain't listening.

MARLON BRANDO

✳

Television is the first truly democratic culture—the first culture available to everybody and entirely governed by what the people want. The most terrifying thing is what the people do want.

CLIVE BARNES, DRAMA CRITIC

✳

I hate television. I hate it as much as peanuts. But I can't stop eating peanuts.

ORSON WELLES, ACTOR, DIRECTOR, PRODUCER, AND WRITER

I would just like to mention Robert Houdini, who in the eighteenth century invented the vanishing-birdcage trick and the theater matinee—may he rot and perish. Good afternoon.

ORSON WELLES (ADDRESSING THE AUDIENCE
AT THE END OF A MATINEE PERFORMANCE)

✳

Everyone denies I am a genius—but nobody ever called me one!

ORSON WELLES (ATTRIBUTED)

It is all very well to be able to write books, but can you waggle your ears?
—J. M. BARRIE, PLAYWRIGHT AND NOVELIST
(SAID TO H. G. WELLS)

✳ ✳ ✳

Bogart's a helluva nice guy till 11:30 p.m. After that he thinks he's Bogart.

DAVE CHAUSEN, RESTAURATEUR

✳

As a kisser, Bogart set an awful example. His mouth addressed a woman's lips with the quivering nibble of a horse closing in on an apple.

LANCE MORROW, JOURNALIST

Directing her was like directing Lassie. You needed fourteen takes to get each one of them right.
OTTO PREMINGER, FILM DIRECTOR AND PRODUCER (REFERRING TO DIRECTING MARILYN MONROE; ATTRIBUTED)

✻

A flock of beetle-brained windsuckers with necks hinged so they can say yes to Darryl Zanuck.
S. J. PERELMAN, HUMORIST (SAID OF THE HOLLYWOOD SET)

✳ ✳ ✳

Television is an invention that permits you to be entertained in your living room by people you wouldn't have in your home.
—DAVID FROST, TV PERSONALITY

✳ ✳ ✳

All the personality of a paper cup.
RAYMOND CHANDLER, WRITER (SAID OF HOLLYWOOD)

✻

The media, far from being a conspiracy to dull the political sense of the people, could be viewed as a conspiracy to disguise the extent of political indifference.

DAVID RIESMAN, SOCIOLOGIST

✻

Hanging is too good for a man who makes puns: he should be drawn and quoted.

FRED ALLEN, COMEDIAN

Imitation is the sincerest form of television.

FRED ALLEN

*

Ten million dollars' worth of intricate and ingenious machinery functioning elaborately to put skin on baloney.

GEORGE JEAN NATHAN, CRITIC, AUTHOR, AND EDITOR
(SAID OF HOLLYWOOD)

*

For an actress to be a success she must have the face of Venus, the brains of Minerva, the grace of Terpsichore, the memory of Macaulay, the figure of Juno, and the hide of a rhinoceros.

ETHEL BARRYMORE, ACTRESS

There is one thing on earth more
terrible than English music, and that
is English painting.
—HEINRICH HEINE, POET

* * *

A critic is a bundle of biases held loosely together by a sense of taste.

WHITNEY BALLIETT, WRITER

* * *

If they can take it for ten minutes,
then play it for fifteen. That's our policy.
Always leave them wanting less.
—ANDY WARHOL,
ARTIST AND FILMMAKER

* * *

People will cross the road at the risk of losing their own lives in order to say, "We saw you on the telly."

QUENTIN CRISP, WRITER,
ACTOR, AND RACONTEUR

*

TV . . . is our latest medium—we call it a medium because nothing's well done.

GOODMAN ACE,
RADIO AND TV WRITER AND COMEDIAN

*

It's very hard for an actor to open his gob without whatever he says sounding risible. If you even whisper a murmur of complaint, you're labeled a po-faced bastard who can't see the funny side of things.

KENNETH BRANAGH,
ACTOR AND FILM DIRECTOR (ATTRIBUTED)

Theater director: a person engaged by the management to conceal the fact that the players cannot act.

JAMES AGATE,
FILM AND DRAMA CRITIC (ATTRIBUTED)

Movies are an inherently stupid art form that often relies on scams, tricks, stunts, gambits, ploys, ruses, or gags that are logically or physically impossible, and often both.

JOE QUEENAN,
JOURNALIST AND WRITER

❋

Between 1956 and 1969, Elvis Presley, in his spare time from being the biggest rock 'n' roll star of all time, managed to make thirty-one of the worst movies in motion-picture history.

JOE QUEENAN

❋

A good storyteller is a person who has a good memory and hopes other people haven't.

IRVINE S. COBB,
HUMORIST AND JOURNALIST (ATTRIBUTED)

O! it offends me to the soul to hear a robus-
tious periwig-pated fellow tear a passion to
tatters, to very rags, to split the ears of the
groundlings, who for the most part are capable
of nothing but inexplicable dumb-shows and
noise: I would have such a fellow whipped for
o'erdoing Termagant; it out-herods Herod:
pray you, avoid it.
—William Shakespeare, from *Hamlet*, act 3, scene 2
(Hamlet is grumpily instructing his players)

* * *

*I'm always amazed that people will actually choose to sit in front of the
television and just be savaged by stuff that belittles their intelligence.*

Alice Walker, novelist and poet

*

*The words, "Kiss Kiss Bang Bang," which I saw on an Italian movie
poster, are perhaps the briefest statement imaginable of the basic appeal
of movies.*

Pauline Kael, film critic

Hollywood will rot on the windmills of Eternity
Hollywood whose movies stick in the throat of God
Yes Hollywood will get what it deserves.

Allen Ginsberg, poet

✶

It's just like having a license to print your own money.

Lord Thomson of Fleet, newspaper owner (talking about
television)

✶

*Why should people go out and pay money to see bad movies when they
can stay at home and see bad television for nothing?*

Samuel Goldwyn, film producer

✶ ✶ ✶

His ears make him look like a taxicab with both doors open.

—Howard Hughes, film producer and business
executive (talking about Clark Gable; attributed)

✶ ✶ ✶

The Merits of Being a Grumpy Old Pessimist,

or

Why It Makes Sense to Think the Worst Will Always Happen

---

*Always borrow money from a pessimist—
he doesn't expect to be paid back.*

—Anonymous

By their very nature, most miserable old bastards have a propensity for pessimism—indeed, they wouldn't know what to do with themselves if they didn't have the freedom to emit a regular flow of gloomy whines across an endless range of subjects. Sample gripes (which should be delivered in suitably lugubrious tones) include:

"I'd better take my umbrella with me because I'm bound to get soaked if I leave the house without one . . . even though rain hasn't been forecast."

"I was standing in that line for five minutes until someone looked up and noticed me—I may as well be invisible."

"There's absolutely no point in my applying for that job because I probably won't even get an interview."

"I don't know why I even have a phone because nobody ever bothers to call me."

"Why should I bother buying a lottery ticket every week? I'm never going to win anything."

"Why is it always me who has to walk the dog?"

Although it's true to say that such a consistently negative attitude rarely generates much sympathy in others, at least if you expect the worst is always certain to happen, then it's a bit of a surprise when something actually works out in your favor. Equally, if you expect the worst to happen, and it does, you don't have to bear the disappointment of having your hopes ground mercilessly into the ground. Every cloud, eh?

Quotable Querulous Quibbles about Pessimism

We all agree that pessimism is a mark of superior intellect.

John Kenneth Galbraith, economist

✳

A pessimist thinks that everybody is as nasty as himself, and hates them for it.

George Bernard Shaw, playwright and writer

✳

The most prolific period of pessimism comes at twenty-one, or thereabouts, when the first attempt is made to translate dreams into reality.

Heywood Broun, journalist

✳ ✳ ✳

Some people are so fond of ill luck that they run halfway to meet it.
—Douglas Jerrold, writer

✳ ✳ ✳

The optimist proclaims that we live in the best of all possible worlds; and the pessimist fears this is true.

James Branch Cabell, author

I'm a pessimist because of intelligence, but an optimist because of will.
Antonio Gramsci, Marxist thinker and activist

*

The nice part about being a pessimist is that you are constantly being either proven right or pleasantly surprised.
George F. Will, columnist and commentator

*

An optimist laughs to forget. A pessimist forgets to laugh.
Anonymous

*

Pessimist: one who, when he has the choice of two evils, chooses both.
Oscar Wilde, playwright and poet

*

My pessimism goes to the point of suspecting the sincerity of the pessimists.
Edmond Rostand, playwright

*

A pessimist is one who builds dungeons in the air.
Walter Winchell, newspaper and radio commentator

* * *

A pessimist is a man who has been compelled to live with an optimist.
—Elbert Hubbard, writer, publisher, and editor

* * *

A pessimist sees only the dark side of the clouds, and mopes; a philosopher sees both sides, and shrugs; an optimist doesn't see the clouds at all—he's walking on them.
—LEONARD LOUIS LEVINSON, WRITER

✳ ✳ ✳

An optimist stays up until midnight to see the new year in. A pessimist stays up to make sure the old year leaves.

BILL VAUGHAN, JOURNALIST AND AUTHOR

✳

The optimist says, "My cup runneth over, what a blessing." The pessimist says, "My cup runneth over, what a mess."

ANONYMOUS

✳

An optimist is merely an ex-pessimist with his pockets full of money, his digestion in good condition, and his wife in the country.

HELEN ROWLAND, WRITER

Both optimists and pessimists contribute
to our society. The optimist invents the
airplane and the pessimist the parachute.
—Gil Stern, writer

*A pessimist is a man who thinks all women are bad. An optimist is a
man who hopes they are.*

Chauncey Mitchell Depew, politician and wit

✳

An optimist is a guy that has never had much experience.

Don Marquis, writer and humorist

✳

The place where optimism most flourishes is the lunatic asylum.

Havelock Ellis, sexologist

✳

Pessimism, when you get used to it, is just as agreeable as optimism.

Arnold Bennett, writer

✳

Rantings of a
Miserable Old Bastard:
Part 2

This section bemoans political correctness. You never see it described as mere "political correctness" these days: it's always "political correctness gone mad." PCGM, we've called it.

- Government agencies, and the buildings that house them, not to mention shopping malls, the media, and advertisers, have embraced an unholy war on Christmas. In the questionable effort not to offend anyone, these champions of political correctness have completely overstepped their bounds and stripped Christian children (as well as children of numerous other denominations who also reap the benefits of this mother-of-all-gift-giving holidays) of the wonder and magic that surrounds—we'll say it!—Christmas!

  Have they gone stark raving mad? Have we reached a point where we can no longer accept the beliefs of others if they happen to be different from our own? To Christians, Christmas is the second of two significant annual celebrations, while to nonbelievers, it's merely a time of celebration, holidays, and merrymaking. Let's leave it at that, and avoid offending Christians even worse by attempting to deny its very existence.

- Some perfectly serviceable words that have been a part of our lexicon since *forever* have been deemed offensive in recent times. These words are perfectly legitimate, descriptive, and *much* shorter than their anemic—but politically correct—cousins. Some examples: homeless person (bum), visually oriented (deaf), person of substance (fat), sanitation engineer (janitor), sex care provider (prostitute), food server (waitress), rhythmically challenged young person (white boy), street activity index (crime  rate). C'mon everybody! Let's go back to being clear and concise. Go on—call that sexually focused, chronologically gifted individual a dirty old man!

- Teachers at one primary school were recently told to stop using red ink when marking their pupils' work because of its "negative connotations." They were advised to use green ink instead. Perhaps the change in policy arose from a concern that their young charges might be scarred for life from being subjected to the horrors of the dreaded red pen. Get used to it, kids—life's a bitch, and then you die . . .

Out of the Mouths of Babes,
or
Why Children Should Be Fried,
Put in Casseroles, or Both

---

*Two things should be cut:
the second act and the child's throat.*

—Noël Coward, playwright and actor
(referring to a child actor)

Let's get one thing straight right from the start. We are not talking only about *your* children in this section, dear reader, even though your own may be naughty little brats at times. No, we are talking chiefly about *other people's* children (although you may recognize yours here somewhere), as it's mostly other people's children who turn you into a grump and tend to bring out the miserable old bastard in you.

For a start, there are too many of them. Children in general, that is, not just the little devils who pull your flowers up and speak obscenities into their cell phones when they're standing right next to you. In bygone days, it made sense to produce lots of the little devils in order to survive, but not anymore.

When very young they have a propensity for making noises, smells, and messes at both ends, making you wish you could have them officially declared antisocial and send them off somewhere. Children are mad. They need to see a shrink. They need to be put out of *our* misery. Then they begin to cultivate zits, creating fascinating facial patterns in which you can make out Ursa Minor, the Pleiades, and the Big Dipper, and they insist on dressing in loose, baggy, unattractive clothes no normal person would be caught dead in. And when they reach their teens, they start to roam shopping malls in hoodies and huge athletic shoes, frightening old ladies who think they're marauding hobbits.

And why can't they talk properly? They go around saying "innit?" and "sweet" and "cool," "like," and "right?" Or they just grunt and look morose. If you're an adult—especially a parent—as far as they're concerned you might as well be from another planet. You've fed them, clothed them, had your house trashed by them, and they loathe you for it.

Doesn't it make you grumpy *when . . .*

. . . you go out with friends for a meal at a local restaurant, and the table next to yours is given to a family with a minimum of two screaming kids in tow? Not only can you no longer hear yourselves over the escalating din at the adjoining table, but there's almost nothing you can do to resolve the situation: if you complain, you'll simply become the bad guy. It's better to wait until one child stabs its sibling with a fork, thus requiring a hasty visit to the emergency room . . . or is that just wishful thinking?

These days, of course, kids aren't happy unless they've got a gadget—and it's usually something noisy that will go out of fashion in about six minutes, when they'll demand (without grace) and usually receive (without gratitude) the next upgrade, whether it's a cell phone, iPod, or computer.

Not only can kids be annoying, but their parents have a tendency to be irritating as well, especially at certain times of the day. Take, for example, the school rush hour: it's easy to forget about it until you find yourself caught up in a sea of SUVs, sporty BMWs, and oversized people carriers (usually containing a single small child), all hogging the roads in an effort to pick up or drop off their little dears in the most aggressive manner possible. What hope have the kids got with parents like that?

It would seem we're not alone in expressing one or two mild reservations about kids. There are a number of others who find these spawn of the Devil less than endearing, too . . .

QUOTABLE QUERULOUS QUIBBLES
ABOUT KIDS

I love children—especially when they cry, for then someone takes them away.

NANCY MITFORD, WRITER (ATTRIBUTED)

✳

The young always have the same problem—how to rebel and conform at the same time. They have now solved this by defying their parents and copying one another.

QUENTIN CRISP, WRITER, ACTOR, AND RACONTEUR

✳ ✳ ✳

Children aren't happy with nothing to ignore,
And that's what parents were created for.
—OGDEN NASH, POET AND HUMORIST

✳ ✳ ✳

I love all my children, but some of them I don't like.

LILLIAN CARTER, NURSE AND
MOTHER OF PRESIDENT JIMMY CARTER

* * *

Sometimes when I look at my children
I say to myself, "Lillian, you should
have stayed a virgin."
—LILLIAN CARTER

* * *

Children and babies should be where they belong—at home, in nurseries, in casseroles.

JIM DUCKER, WRITER (SAID OF KIDS IN RESTAURANTS)

*

When childhood dies, its corpses are called adults and they enter society, one of the politer names of hell. That is why we dread children, even if we love them. They show us the state of our decay.

BRIAN ALDISS, SCIENCE FICTION WRITER

*

I like children—fried.

W. C. FIELDS, ACTOR AND COMEDIAN

*

It is . . . sometimes easier to head an institute for the study of child guidance than it is to turn one brat into a decent human being.

JOSEPH WOOD KRUTCH, ESSAYIST AND NATURALIST

It was no wonder that people were so horrible when they started life as children.

KINGSLEY AMIS, NOVELIST

* * *

Schoolchildren are like normal children only psychotic. They are armed, dangerous, violent, rude, unkempt and obsessed with smoking behind the bike sheds.

—DAVID QUANTICK, COMEDIAN AND WRITER

* * *

The nice thing about having relatives' kids around is that they go home.

CLIFF RICHARD, POP SINGER

*

People treat children as though there's something wrong with them because they're ignorant and small. They say, "I'm so worried about Alexander's development. I mean, he's got no grasp of bonded numbers, no concept of phonics, his hand-to-eye coordination is all over the place. I mean, goodness knows what he's going to be like when he's born."

JEREMY HARDY, COMEDIAN

*

My theory is, children should be born without parents—if born they must be.

LANGSTON HUGHES, NOVELIST,
PLAYWRIGHT, AND SHORT-STORY WRITER

Never have children, only grandchildren.

GORE VIDAL, NOVELIST AND ESSAYIST

✳

*The real menace in dealing with a five-year-old is that in no time at all
you begin to sound like a five-year-old.*

JEAN KERR, PLAYWRIGHT AND HUMORIST

There was a little girl
Who had a little curl
Right in the middle of her forehead;
When she was good
She was very very good,
But when she was bad she was horrid.
—HENRY WADSWORTH LONGFELLOW, POET

* * *

The thing that best defines a child is the total inability to receive information from anything not plugged in.

BILL COSBY, ACTOR, AUTHOR, AND COMEDIAN

✳

There is no more somber enemy of good art than the pram in the hall.

CYRIL CONNOLLY, WRITER AND JOURNALIST

✳

They never lynch children, babies, no matter what they do, they are whitewashed in advance.

SAMUEL BECKETT, PLAYWRIGHT, NOVELIST, AND POET (FROM *The Expelled and Other Novellas*)

✳ ✳ ✳

All God's children are not beautiful. Most of God's children are, in fact, barely presentable.

—FRAN LEBOWITZ, JOURNALIST

✳ ✳ ✳

Fooling All of the People,
or
Why Politicians Are Held in Such Contempt

*If presidents don't do it to their wives,
they do it to the country.*
—MEL BROOKS, FILM DIRECTOR

How do you know when politicians are lying? Simple— their lips are moving. In fact the only time you can be sure that politicians are telling the truth is when they're calling each other "liar." To most people they're just a bunch of slimy, devious, scheming, underhanded, conniving, self-seeking, cheating, fraudulent crooks.

What's most annoying is that there isn't a constant or regular appraisal that keeps them on their toes in their cozy little ivory towers either. In industry, you make money for your bosses or you're out, but in politics, provided you can keep pulling the wool over the eyes of your constituents and ask enough questions in Congress to appear to be doing something, you're safe. The weak last a long time in politics.

Did you hear the one about the guy who was having a brain transplant? The surgeon says, "We've got the brain of a polymath—a man who was well versed in the sciences, the arts, the humanities, and he was a Nobel winner to boot. That'll cost you fifty grand. Then there's this one from a politician. That'll knock you back a hundred grand." When the guy asks why the politician's brain is twice as expensive, the surgeon replies, "Because it's never been used."

Politicians? You can keep 'em. Whatever the party. We make no excuses for ranting about the ones that are currently in power, but they're all just as bad, and if the other party was in power, we'd probably be saying much the same. But enough of our futile whining—let's look at what others have had to say about this loathsome species . . .

QUOTABLE QUERULOUS QUIBBLES ABOUT POLITICS

The trouble with this country is that there are too many politicians who believe, with a conviction based on experience, that you can fool all of the people all of the time.
—FRANKLIN P. ADAMS, JOURNALIST AND RADIO PERSONALITY (AN ALLUSION TO LINCOLN'S FREQUENTLY QUOTED "YOU MAY FOOL ALL THE PEOPLE SOME OF THE TIME; YOU CAN EVEN FOOL SOME OF THE PEOPLE ALL THE TIME; BUT YOU CAN'T FOOL ALL THE PEOPLE ALL THE TIME.")

Politicians are like diapers: they should be changed often—and for the same reason.

BARRY CRYER, COMEDIAN

✳ ✳ ✳

When the politicians complain that TV turns their proceedings into a circus, it should be made plain that the circus was already there, and that TV has merely demonstrated that not all the performers are well trained.

—ED MURROW, JOURNALIST (ATTRIBUTED)

✳ ✳ ✳

Any man who is under thirty, and is not a liberal, has no heart; and any man who is over thirty, and is not a conservative, has no brains.

WINSTON CHURCHILL, BRITISH PRIME MINISTER

✳

A sheep in sheep's clothing.

WINSTON CHURCHILL (SAID OF LABOR'S PRIME MINISTER CLEMENT ATTLEE)

✳

Political skill . . . the ability to foretell what is going to happen tomorrow, next week, next month, and next year. And to have the ability afterwards to explain why it didn't happen.

WINSTON CHURCHILL

In war you can only be killed once, but in politics—many times.

WINSTON CHURCHILL (ATTRIBUTED)

✳

Politics is not the art of the possible. It consists in choosing between the disastrous and the unpalatable.

JOHN KENNETH GALBRAITH,
ECONOMIST ("POLITICS IS THE ART
OF THE POSSIBLE" IS ATTRIBUTED
TO THE NINETEENTH-CENTURY
GERMAN STATESMAN
PRINCE OTTO VON BISMARCK)

✳

Nothing is so admirable in politics as a short memory.

JOHN KENNETH GALBRAITH

✳

There are times in politics when you must be on the right side and lose.

JOHN KENNETH GALBRAITH

✳ ✳ ✳

Democracy consists of choosing your dictators, after they've told you what you think it is you want to hear.

—ALAN COREN, HUMORIST

✳ ✳ ✳

There is one rule for politicians all over the world: don't say in power what you say in opposition; if you do, you only have to carry out what the other fellows have found impossible.

John Galsworthy, novelist and playwright

*

A group of politicians deciding to dump a president because his morals are bad is like the Mafia getting together to bump off the godfather for not going to church on Sunday.

Russell Baker, humorist

*

Alliance, n.: *in international politics, the union of two thieves who have their hands so deeply inserted into each other's pocket that they cannot safely plunder a third.*

Battle, n.: *a method of untying with the teeth a political knot that will not yield to the tongue.*

Conservative, n.: *a statesman who is enamored of existing evils, as distinguished from the Liberal who wishes to replace them with others.*

History, n.: *an account, mostly false, of events, mostly unimportant, which are brought about by rulers, mostly knaves, and soldiers, mostly fools.*

Opposition, n.: *in politics the party that prevents the government from running amuck by hamstringing it.*

Politics, n.: *a strife of interests masquerading as a contest of principles.*

Referendum, n.: *a law for submission of proposed legislation to a popular vote to learn the nonsensus of public opinion.*

Ambrose Bierce, writer and journalist

Politics are for foreigners with their endless wrongs and paltry rights. Politics are a lousy way to get things done. Politics are, like God's infinite mercy, a last resort.
—P. J. O'ROURKE, SATIRIST AND JOURNALIST

* * *

Hell, I never vote for anybody. I always vote against.

W. C. FIELDS, ACTOR AND COMEDIAN

Why should I question the monkey, when I can question the organ grinder?

ANEURIN BEVAN, POLITICIAN (PREFERRING TO QUESTION BRITISH PRIME MINISTER WINSTON CHURCHILL RATHER THAN THE FOREIGN SECRETARY)

And you call that statesmanship.
I call it an emotional spasm.
—Aneurin Bevan (speaking at a conference
of the British Labor Party)

✳ ✳ ✳

What do you want to be a sailor for? There are greater storms in politics than you will ever find at sea. Piracy, broadsides, blood on the decks. You will find them all in politics.

David Lloyd George,
British prime minister

✳

I have come to the conclusion that politics is too serious a matter to be left to the politicians.

Charles de Gaulle, French president,
soldier, and statesman

✳

Since a politician never believes what he says, he is surprised when others believe him.

Charles de Gaulle

✳

It's a great country, where anybody can grow up to be president—except me.

Barry Goldwater,
politician

VIC OLIVER *(Churchill's son-in-law): Who, in your opinion, is the greatest statesman you know?*

CHURCHILL *(smartly): Benito Mussolini.*

OLIVER: *What? Why?*

CHURCHILL: *Mussolini is the only statesman who had the requisite courage to have his son-in-law executed.*

(SARAH CHURCHILL'S MARRIAGE TO THE MUCH OLDER COMEDIAN DID NOT LAST LONG.)

*

Politics is perhaps the only profession for which no preparation is thought necessary.

ROBERT LOUIS STEVENSON, NOVELIST, ESSAYIST, AND POET

A Conservative government is an organized hypocrisy.
—BENJAMIN DISRAELI,
BRITISH PRIME MINISTER AND WRITER

* * *

A week is a long time in politics.
—Harold Wilson,
British prime minister

✳ ✳ ✳

I hate politics and the belief in politics, because it makes men arrogant, doctrinaire, obstinate, and inhuman.

Thomas Mann, writer

✳

In politics, what begins in fear usually ends in folly.

Samuel Taylor Coleridge,
poet, critic, and philosopher

✳

The first thing that one loses in politics is one's freedom.

Joaquim Maria Machado de Assis,
novelist and short-story writer

✳

Politics is opposed to morality, as philosophy to naïvety.

Emmanuel Levinas, philosopher

✳

Any American who is prepared to run for president should automatically, by definition, be disqualified from ever doing so.

Gore Vidal,
novelist and essayist (attributed)

All political lives, unless they are cut off in mid-stream at a happy junc-ture, end in failure, because that is the nature of politics and of human affairs.

ENOCH POWELL, POLITICIAN

✳

The difference between a Democracy and a Dictatorship is that in a Democracy you vote first and take orders later; in a Dictatorship you don't have to waste your time voting.

CHARLES BUKOWSKI,
POET AND AUTHOR

✱ ✱ ✱

He knows nothing and thinks he
knows everything. That points clearly
to a political career.
—GEORGE BERNARD SHAW,
PLAYWRIGHT AND WRITER

✱ ✱ ✱

Christchurch was the place where the difference between the Tories and the Alfred Chicken Party was that members of the Alfred Chicken Party ran around with their heads still on.

PHILIP GOLDENBERG, POLITICIAN
(REFERRING TO A BY-ELECTION THE
BRITISH TORIES UNEXPECTEDLY LOST)

As usual, the Liberals offer a mixture of sound and original ideas. Unfortunately none of the sound ideas is original and none of the original ideas is sound.

HAROLD MACMILLAN,
BRITISH PRIME MINISTER

People never lie so much as after a hunt,
during a war or before an election.
—PRINCE OTTO VON BISMARCK,
GERMAN STATESMAN

✳ ✳ ✳

Politics are usually the executive expression of human immaturity.

VERA BRITTAIN,
PACIFIST AND WRITER

✳

Anyone who wants the presidency so much that he'll spend two years organizing and campaigning for it is not to be trusted with the office.

DAVID BRODER, JOURNALIST

Politics is the art of looking for trouble, finding it, misdiagnosing it, and then misapplying the wrong remedies.

GROUCHO MARX, COMEDIAN

✳

I have always said, the first Whig was the Devil.

SAMUEL JOHNSON, LEXICOGRAPHER, CRITIC, AND ESSAYIST

✳

I fear my Socialism is purely cerebral; I do not like the masses in the flesh.

HAROLD NICOLSON, DIPLOMAT, WRITER, AND CRITIC

✳ ✳ ✳

Under democracy one party always devotes its energies to trying to prove that the other party is unfit to rule—and both commonly succeed and are right.

—H. L. MENCKEN, JOURNALIST, CRITIC, AND EDITOR

✳ ✳ ✳

Rantings of a Miserable Old Bastard: Part 3

Shopping—Why does it always seem to be that after waiting in line in a supermarket for what seems like a week (but is probably about ten minutes), just as you finally reach the front of the line, another register opens up just next door? You're never that lucky when it comes to choosing lines—you try to go for the shortest, in the hope that it'll be the fastest, but it always ends up taking twice as long as all the others. It's as though whichever line you stand in, you'll be certain to jinx it.

MOVIE MISERY—Picture the scene: you're in a movie theater, the film is just about to start and you've got a clear view of the screen . . . until some six-foot-ten-inch giant chooses to sit directly in front of you, thus ruining the evening's entertainment. Another surefire way to be antagonized at the movies is to find yourself sitting in close proximity to a serial muncher who likes nothing more than to extract peppermint candies from deafeningly loud wrappers, slowly, painfully, irritatingly. Even people's popcorn-guzzling antics can be an excruciating distraction.

TRANSPORTATION BLUES—Why is it that, whenever you arrive early at the train station, the train you need to catch is delayed for several minutes or even hours, forcing you to wait in the cold until it turns up; however, on the days when you get to the station just seconds after the train was scheduled to depart, inevitably it has left on time, the doors closing mockingly as you hurl yourself onto the platform in desperation. What is that all about?

MOBILE MADNESS—There are few things worse than having to endure listening to tediously banal cell phone conversations while you're traveling home in the subway or bus after a hard day at work, particularly when all you want to do is sleep or be left in peace to read a book. These people who feel the need to share the tiresome details of their sad little lives (at full volume) with a car full of complete strangers are ignorant, arrogant, or just plain selfish. Oh to have the courage to swipe the offending phone from the offensive passenger's hand and toss it through an open window onto the opposite track . . . One day, perhaps.

TRACTOR TEDIUM—How annoying is it to be driving casually along scenic country roads only to end up stuck behind a rambling, manure-carrying tractor that shows no immediate sign of turning off the winding "main" road? Invariably the route is littered with blind corners and dangerous bends so that passing the tractor is completely out of the question. No, instead you have to take a deep breath, slow down, and fall in behind the hulking heap of metal until, after a two-mile crawl, it stops splattering your windscreen with fragments of its stinking load and leaves the road for good.

Quotable Insights into Misery

Most people spend the greater part of their lives making others miserable.

JEAN DE LA BRUYÈRE, WRITER

✳

We become moral once we are miserable.

MARCEL PROUST, NOVELIST AND CRITIC

✳

The secret of being miserable is to have leisure to bother about whether you are happy or not. The cure for it is occupation.

GEORGE BERNARD SHAW, PLAYWRIGHT AND WRITER

✳ ✳ ✳

Most people would rather be certain they're miserable, than risk being happy.
—ROBERT ANTHONY, SELF-HELP AUTHOR

✳ ✳ ✳

Friends love misery, in fact. Sometimes, especially if we are too lucky or too successful or too pretty, our misery is the only thing that endears us to our friends.

ERICA JONG, NOVELIST AND POET

The minute you leave your house in the morning you see something that makes you grumpy.

ARTHUR SMITH, WRITER AND COMEDIAN

* * *

What fresh hell is this?
—DOROTHY PARKER,
HUMORIST, CRITIC, AND WRITER
(ON THE MORNING MAIL DELIVERY)

The sneeze in English is the harbinger of misery, even death. I sometimes think the only pleasure a person has is in passing on his cold germs.

GERALD DURRELL,
NATURALIST AND WRITER

*

The misery of a child is interesting to a mother, the misery of a young man is interesting to a young woman, the misery of an old man is interesting to nobody.

VICTOR HUGO, POET,
NOVELIST, AND PLAYWRIGHT

Just because you're miserable doesn't mean you can't enjoy your life.

ANNETTE GOODHEART, WRITER

*

A man's as miserable as he thinks he is.

SENECA, ROMAN PHILOSOPHER,
MID-FIRST CENTURY CE

*

*Those who have had great passions
often find all their lives made miserable
in being cured of them.*

FRANÇOIS DE LA ROCHEFOUCAULD, AUTHOR

* * *

Money, if it does not bring you happiness,
will at least help you be miserable
in comfort.

—HELEN GURLEY BROWN, EDITOR AND WRITER

* * *

Nation Shall Speak Insults unto Nation,
or
Foreign Bodies and Why Decent People Don't Like Them

Hell is a place where the motorists are French, the policemen are German, and the cooks are English.
—ANONYMOUS

All right, so some people might consider terms such as "Rednecks" for Americans, "Frogs" for the French, "Limeys" for the British, and "Krauts" for Germans as somewhat offensive, but where's their sense of humor? Let's not get so depressingly politically correct about this. *Vive la différence!* We are what we are—and everyone else is . . . well, foreign.

Not that we think they're inferior, of course. We certainly wouldn't *dream* of saying that. Not even of the French. Well, not much. No, they're just something else. Other. Unfamiliar. Alien. And we know how much they enjoy a laugh at our expense, so why shouldn't we do the same to them?

But Europe? Don't get us started on Europe. The issue is not Europe the continent, but Europe the European Union. There they are, as diverse a bunch of nations as you can get, and they want to keep making it bigger, still believing that they'll continue to get along like happy old friends on an annual trip to Miami.

Did you know that, in 2003, trapeze artists and jugglers with the Moscow State Circus were told they would have to wear hard hats during a tour of the United Kingdom to comply with European Union safety rules? Whether they obeyed the idiotic ruling is not known for certain, but it was introduced nevertheless. Apart from making them look utterly ridiculous, surely wearing such bulky headgear could result in more accidents, with performers struggling to maintain a straight face opposite colleagues who look as though they've just stepped off a building site.

Doesn't it make you grumpy *when* . . .

. . . you've traveled to France with the express intention of improving your knowledge of the French language, and yet whenever you try to make the effort to converse with a local, especially in Paris, your earnest attempts are met with withering disdain and a mockingly condescending reply in English?

As for us, can Americans still be called oversexed? Not anymore, because we're all too fat. Overpaid? You can say that again—you've only got to look at the size of the cars we drive to see that.

And what an arrogant, loudmouthed bunch we are, with our gas-guzzling ways, our lack of patience, our zealous Christianity, and our teeth. If you can't tell if a guy's American, count his teeth—all pristine white and neatly lined up like a row of porcelain urinals. And why does every American you see on TV seem to have an analyst? Are we all mad? Well, obviously. Admitting that we're several states short of a Union seems to be part of our psyche.

Doesn't it make you grumpy *when* . . .

. . . you are confronted by far too many choices, particularly when it comes to ordering food? Nothing is ever straightforward or plain. Burgers come in 101 different ways; it's impossible to order just a simple, plain coffee; there must be fifteen kinds of salad dressing at any given restaurant. And the portions? You could feed a European family of four on the contents of one meal alone. It's a wonder America hasn't sunk under the weight of its hefty occupants.

As for the Aussies—well. They can't make a statement (you know, a straightforward sentence in the indicative mood?) or give a command (using the verb imperatively?) without seeming to ask a question (that is, using an interrogative). You never know whether they're telling you something or asking you something, with that little inflection at the end of *every single*

sentence. It's just as well they're on the other side of the world. Although that didn't stop them from imposing the Bee Gees on us, or Kylie Minogue, or their inferior wine.

But enough criticism about our foreign cousins, because it is also true that many like to turn their back on patriotic feelings in favor of taking a grumpy old sideswipe at their own country and native peoples. We've found a selection of quotable quibbles to prove it.

Quotable Querulous Quibbles about Nationality

The English instinctively admire any man who has no talent and is modest about it.

James Agate, film and drama critic

✳ ✳ ✳

Poor Mexico, so far from God and so close to the United States.
—Porfirio Díaz, Mexican president, statesman, and soldier

✳ ✳ ✳

Curse the blasted, jelly-boned swines, the slimy, the belly-wriggling invertebrates, the miserable sodding rotters, the flaming sods, the snivelling, dribbling, dithering, palsied, pulse-less lot that make up England today. They've got white of egg in their veins, and their spunk is that watery it's a marvel they can breed.

D. H. Lawrence, novelist and poet (in a letter)

In America, only the successful writer is important, in France all writers are important, in England no writer is important, and in Australia you have to explain what a writer is.

GEOFFREY COTTRELL, WRITER

✳

Germans are flummoxed by humor, the Swiss have no concept of fun, the Spanish think there is nothing at all ridiculous about eating dinner at midnight, and the Italians should never, ever have been let in on the invention of the motor car.

BILL BRYSON, WRITER

✳

The English think that incompetence is the same thing as sincerity.
QUENTIN CRISP, WRITER, ACTOR, AND RACONTEUR

✳

If you're going to America, bring your own food.

FRAN LEBOWITZ, JOURNALIST

✳

The Englishman is never content but when he is grumbling.

SCOTTISH SAYING

✳ ✳ ✳

Canada could have had French culture, American know-how, and English government. Instead it got French government, English know-how, and American culture.

JOHN COLOMBO, WRITER

✳ ✳ ✳

We know of no spectacle so ridiculous as the British public in one of its periodical fits of morality.

THOMAS BABINGTON MACAULAY,
HISTORIAN AND ESSAYIST

✻

The French are a logical people, which is one reason the English dislike them so intensely. The other is that they own France, a country which we have always judged to be much too good for them.

ROBERT MORLEY, ACTOR

I look upon Switzerland as an inferior sort of Scotland.
—SYDNEY SMITH, WRITER AND WIT

✻ ✻ ✻

Scotland: that garret of the earth, that knuckle-end of England, that land of Calvin, oatcakes, and sulfur.

SYDNEY SMITH

Britain is the only country in the world where the food is more dangerous than the sex.
—JACKIE MASON, COMEDIAN

✳ ✳ ✳

American history is perceived by most people as a luxury, an entertainment at best, and at worst, an escape from the present.

CARL N. DEGLER, HISTORIAN

✳

There have been many definitions of hell, but for the English the best definition is that it is the place where the Germans are the police, the Swedish are the comedians, the Italians are the defense force, Frenchmen dig the roads, the Belgians are the pop singers, the Spanish run the railways, the Turks cook the food, the Irish are the waiters, the Greeks run the government, and the common language is Dutch.

DAVID FROST, TV PERSONALITY, AND ANTHONY JAY, WRITER AND JOURNALIST (IN *To England with Love*)

✳

The French are wiser than they seem, and the Spaniards seem wiser than they are.

FRANCIS BACON, STATESMAN AND PHILOSOPHER

✳

In Russia a man is called reactionary if he objects to having his property stolen and his wife and children murdered.

WINSTON CHURCHILL, BRITISH PRIME MINISTER

Americans always try to do the right thing—after they've tried every-thing else.

WINSTON CHURCHILL

✳

All the faces here this evening seem to be bloody Poms.

PRINCE CHARLES, HEIR APPARENT TO THE BRITISH THRONE (SAID AT AN AUSTRALIA DAY DINNER)

The French complain of everything, and always.
—NAPOLÉON BONAPARTE,
FRENCH EMPEROR

✳ ✳ ✳

Basically the French are all peasants.

PABLO PICASSO, PAINTER

✳

Some people may be Rooshans, and others may be Prooshans; they are born so, and will please themselves. Them which is of other natures thinks different.

CHARLES DICKENS, NOVELIST
(SAID BY MRS. GAMP IN *Martin Chuzzlewit*)

Their demeanor is invariably morose, sullen, clownish and repulsive. I should think there is not, on the face of the earth, a people so entirely destitute of humor, vivacity, or the capacity for enjoyment.

CHARLES DICKENS (ABOUT AMERICANS)

※

The 100 per cent American is 99 per cent idiot.

GEORGE BERNARD SHAW, PLAYWRIGHT AND WRITER

※

I fear that I have not got much to say about Canada, not having seen much; what I got by going to Canada was a cold.

HENRY DAVID THOREAU,
WRITER, PHILOSOPHER, AND NATURALIST

Of course, America had often been discovered before Columbus, but it had always been hushed up.

OSCAR WILDE, PLAYWRIGHT AND POET

※

America is one long expectoration.

OSCAR WILDE

Other people have a nationality.
The Irish and the Jews have a psychosis.
—Brendan Behan,
PLAYWRIGHT AND AUTHOR

✳ ✳ ✳

The English think soap is civilization.
Heinrich von Treitschke, historian and political writer

✳

Canada is a country so square that even the female impersonators are women.

Richard Brenner, actor

English coffee tastes like water that has been squeezed out of a wet sleeve.

Fred Allen, comedian

✳

I know why the sun never sets on the British Empire: God wouldn't trust an Englishman in the dark.

Duncan Spaeth, university professor

Americans are possibly the dumbest people on the planet. . . . We Americans suffer from an enforced ignorance. We don't know about anything that's happening outside our country. Our stupidity is embarrassing.

Michael Moore, filmmaker

*

French Canada is a relic of the historical past preserved by isolation, as Siberian mammoths are preserved by ice.

Goldwin Smith, historian and journalist

*

What is not clear is not French; what is not clear is, moreover, English, Italian, Greek, or Latin.

Antoine de Rivarol, eighteenth-century journalist and critic

*

English physicians kill you, the French let you die.

Lord Melbourne, British prime minister

* * *

All Frenchmen want to encroach and extend their territorial possessions at the expense of other nations. Their rarity prompts them to be the first nation in the world.

—Lord Palmerston,
British prime minister

* * *

*Americans can eat garbage, provided you sprinkle it liberally with
ketchup, mustard, chilli sauce, Tabasco sauce, cayenne pepper, or any
other condiment which destroys the original flavor of the dish.*

HENRY MILLER, NOVELIST AND CRITIC

Boy, those French: they have a different word for everything!

STEVE MARTIN, FILM ACTOR

Imagine the Lord talking French!
Aside from a few odd words in Hebrew,
I took it completely for granted that God
had never spoken anything but the most
dignified English.

—CLARENCE SHEPARD DAY, WRITER

* * *

Food isolates the French almost as much as their language. That would not be serious if France were at least certain of remaining a refuge for good food.

THEODORE ZELDIN, HISTORIAN

✳ ✳ ✳

Never criticize Americans. They have the best taste that money can buy.

—MILES KINGTON,
WRITER AND JOURNALIST

✳ ✳ ✳

The Englishman who has lost his fortune is said to have died of a broken heart.

RALPH WALDO EMERSON, POET AND ESSAYIST

✳

German is the most extravagantly ugly language—it sounds like someone using a sick bag on a 747.

WILLY RUSHTON, COMEDIAN

A Frenchman must be always talking, whether he knows anything of the matter or not; an Englishman is content to say nothing, when he has nothing to say.

SAMUEL JOHNSON,
LEXICOGRAPHER, CRITIC, AND ESSAYIST

✳

I hate the French because they are all slaves, and wear wooden shoes.

OLIVER GOLDSMITH,
NOVELIST, PLAYWRIGHT, AND POET

✳

In our country we have those three unspeakably precious things: freedom of speech, freedom of conscience, and the prudence to never practice either of them.

MARK TWAIN, WRITER

✳

Germany—the diseased world's bathhouse.

MARK TWAIN

✳

In Paris they simply stared when I spoke to them in French; I never did succeed in making those idiots understand their own language.

MARK TWAIN

✳ ✳ ✳

I can speak French, but I cannot understand it.
—MARK TWAIN

✳ ✳ ✳

The problem with Ireland is that it's a country full of genius, but with absolutely no talent.

HUGH LEONARD, WRITER AND PLAYWRIGHT

✳ ✳ ✳

The French are sawed-off sissies who eat snails and slugs and cheese that smells like people's feet. Utter cowards who force their own children to drink wine, they gibber like baboons even when you try to speak to them in their own wimpy language.

—P. J. O'ROURKE, SATIRIST AND JOURNALIST

✳ ✳ ✳

You can always reason with a German. You can always reason with a barnyard animal, too, for all the good it does.

P. J. O'ROURKE

✳

The Greeks—dirty and impoverished descendants of a bunch of la-de-da fruit salads who invented democracy and then forgot how to use it while walking around dressed up as girls.

P. J. O'ROURKE

✳

France is a country where the money falls apart, but you can't tear the toilet paper.

BILLY WILDER, FILM DIRECTOR, WRITER, AND PRODUCER

The French will only be united under the threat of danger. Nobody can simply bring together a country that has 265 kinds of cheese.
—CHARLES DE GAULLE, FRENCH PRESIDENT, SOLDIER, AND STATESMAN

✳ ✳ ✳

The best thing I know between France and England is the sea.
DOUGLAS JERROLD, WRITER

✳

The German mind has a talent for making no mistakes but the very greatest.
CLIFTON FADIMAN, INTELLECTUAL AND AUTHOR

✳

This is one race of people for whom psychoanalysis is of no use whatsoever.
SIGMUND FREUD, PHYSICIAN AND FOUNDER OF PSYCHOANALYSIS (SAID OF THE IRISH)

✳

No one ever went broke underestimating the taste of the American public.
H. L. MENCKEN, JOURNALIST, CRITIC AND EDITOR

The Japanese have perfected good manners and made them indistinguishable from rudeness.

Paul Theroux, travel writer and novelist

✶

Russians will consume marinated mushrooms and vodka, salted herring and vodka, smoked salmon and vodka, salami and vodka, caviar on brown bread and vodka, pickled cucumbers and vodka, cold tongue and vodka, red beet salad and vodka, scallions and vodka—anything and everything and vodka.

Hedrick Smith, journalist

✶ ✶ ✶

Scotland: a land of meanness, sophistry and lust.
—Lord Byron, poet

The food in Yugoslavia is fine if you like pork tartare.

Ed Begley Jr., TV and film actor

✶

All Englishmen talk as if they've got a bushel of plums stuck in their throats, and then, after swallowing them, get constipated from the pits.

W. C. Fields, actor and comedian

The Information Superidiots
or
Why Were Morons Ever Allowed on the Internet?

A world awash in information is one in which information has very little market value.
—Paul Krugman, economist

Information superhighway? Ha! Whatever the information is, it certainly isn't "super." Not the sort of nonsense you get on the Internet, anyhow. When it was made available to all and sundry several years ago, it promised us so much: shopping online, research, lots to read and do and see, but look at the rubbish that's there—taking up precious bandwidth (or whatever it's called). A random surf came up with a few Web sites that make you wonder why their owners haven't got something better to do. It's enough to make you want to rip your typing fingers off, one by one.

There's a Web cat, apparently, that "sits on your screen and interacts with your mouse." What's the point of that? And while we're on the subject of annoying things to do with computers, Microsoft has produced something called Clippit, which is a maddeningly groveling little paperclip-shaped icon that sits with an inane smile on its face, waiting for you to make a mistake. As soon as you do, it pounces and throws up a totally distracting yellow note on your screen saying, "It looks as if you're about to write a letter. Do you need some help?" No, you exasperating electronic moron, I know how to write letters, thank you very much. Next!

There's a site devoted to pictures of stuff that's been left on the pavement. Among these treasured pix are shots of a prosthetic leg and an inflated rubber glove. Just think how deprived you would be if you never happen across this Web site.

Another site offers you a pet rock. No, not a rockfish or a roc—that large mythical bird from the Arabian Nights—but a heavy bit of hard mineral aggregate. *That* type of rock. The sort of thing you often feel like throwing at your screen, hoping that it magically traverses the superhighway and hits the Web site owner right between the eyes. How sad would you have to be to buy one of these supremely useless objects?

When you've finished having a Socratic discourse with your pet rock, you  can go to a site devoted to practicing origami with toilet paper; or you can be a total sicko and visit a site devoted to plane crashes. "Name That Beard" is a site that lets you— well, name that beard. You look at a beard and decide whether it belongs to Karl Marx, Ernest Hemingway, or Abraham Lincoln. You can also "Ask Satan" a question or match beer bottles to their labels, and there's a site that teaches you how to play air guitar . . .

Quotations about the Internet are few and far between. In fact, so few and far between that what few are to be found are all crap and aren't worth bothering with. Anyway, similar sentiments are expressed among those who moan about technology in general (see the "White Heat and Snake Oil" chapter).

But there is one, and it was penned by Andy, coauthor of this book. It just came to him one day when he was ironing the cat:

> A world once served by gods and heroes
> Now gets by with ones and zeros.

Not bad, even though he does say so himself. But, then, he would.

However, give it ten or twenty years, and there'll be an entire *Bartlett's Guide to Quotations about the Internet from Grumpy Bastards Who Still Live in the World of Inkwells, Blotting Paper, and Hammermill Bond*—a guaranteed best seller, surely?

Battles of the Sexes,
or
What Is It about Men and Women That Makes Them Bitch at One Another?

---

*I believe in tying the marriage knot, as long as
it's around the woman's neck.*

—W. C. FIELDS, ACTOR AND COMEDIAN

What is it about men and women (usually when they've entered coupledom) that they have to be so damned bitchy about? Why can't they just live in harmony?

Perhaps the best solution would be if all couples were of the same-sex variety . . . Until this happens, though, the relentless bickering between husbands and wives, boyfriends and girlfriends, is destined to go on and on and on . . .

There are theories about why men are grumpier than women. There are also theories about why the opposite is apparently true. In 2002, some scientists came up with an explanation for the former, with the conclusion that men were suffering from "irritable-male syndrome." It amounts, they said, to a drop in a middle-aged man's levels of the male hormone testosterone, which duly affects their brains and therefore their behavior. So a conversation like this might be quite commonplace nowadays:

"You're a grumpy fart, aren't you?"

"No, I'm not."

"Yes, you are."

"No, I'm not. My testosterone levels are a bit on the low side today, that's all. It's scientific. Now piss off!"

QUOTABLE QUERULOUS QUIBBLES
ABOUT THE SEXES

Men are those creatures with two legs and eight hands.

JAYNE MANSFIELD, FILM ACTRESS

And a woman is only a woman, but a good cigar is a smoke.

RUDYARD KIPLING, WRITER AND POET

✳

Male, n.: *a member of the unconsidered, or negligible, sex. The male of the human race is commonly known to the female as Mere Man. The genus has two varieties: good providers and bad providers.*

AMBROSE BIERCE, WRITER AND JOURNALIST

✳ ✳ ✳

Marriage—the most advanced form of warfare in the modern world.
—MALCOLM BRADBURY, WRITER

✳ ✳ ✳

All marriages are happy. It's the
living together afterward that causes
all the trouble.
—RAYMOND HULL, WRITER

✳ ✳ ✳

A woman will lie about anything, just to stay in practice.
PHILIP MARLOWE, NOVELIST

✳

*Though marriage makes man and wife one flesh, it leaves 'em still
two fools.*
WILLIAM CONGREVE, PLAYWRIGHT

✳

There are no great men, buster. There are only men.
CHARLES SCHNEE, SCREENWRITER
(FROM HIS 1952 SCREENPLAY *The Bad and the Beautiful*)

✳

A good marriage would be between a blind wife and a deaf husband.
MICHEL DE MONTAIGNE, ESSAYIST

Some of my best leading men have been dogs and horses.
ELIZABETH TAYLOR, ACTRESS

*

Her arms are too fat, her legs are too short, and she is too big in the bust.
RICHARD BURTON, ACTOR
(ON HIS NEW WIFE ELIZABETH TAYLOR)

* * *

The secret of a happy marriage remains a secret.
—HENNY YOUNGMAN, COMEDIAN AND ACTOR

* * *

There is one woman whom fate has destined for each of us. If we miss her we are saved.
ANONYMOUS

* * *

Women want mediocre men, and men are working hard to become as mediocre as possible.
—MARGARET MEAD, ANTHROPOLOGIST

* * *

Marriage is the price men pay for sex;
sex is the price women pay for marriage.
—ANONYMOUS

* * *

Boys will be boys, and so will a lot of middle-aged men.
KIN HUBBARD, HUMORIST

✳

Wedding rings: the world's smallest handcuffs.

ANONYMOUS

✳

Marriage is an arrangement by which two people start by getting the best out of each other and often end by getting the worst.
GERALD BRENAN, WRITER

✳

The more I see of men, the more I admire dogs.
MADAME ROLAND, WRITER (ATTRIBUTED)

It was very good of God to let Carlyle and Mrs. Carlyle marry one another, and so make two people miserable instead of four.

SAMUEL BUTLER, WRITER

✳

Brigands demand your money or your life; women require both.

SAMUEL BUTLER

✳

Bigamy is having one husband too many, monogamy is the same.

QUOTED AS AN EPIGRAPH TO ERICA JONG'S *Fear of Flying*

✳

Once a woman gives you her heart, you can never get rid of the rest of her body.

JOHN VANBRUGH, ARCHITECT AND PLAYWRIGHT

✳ ✳ ✳

Sometimes I wonder if men and women really suit each other. Perhaps they should live next door and just visit now and then.
—KATHARINE HEPBURN, ACTRESS

✳ ✳ ✳

A woman's preaching is like a dog's walking on his hinder legs. It is not done well; but you are surprised to find it done at all.

SAMUEL JOHNSON, LEXICOGRAPHER,
CRITIC, AND ESSAYIST (QUOTED BY
HIS BIOGRAPHER JAMES BOSWELL)

When a man steals your wife, there is no better revenge than to let him keep her.

SACHA GUITRY, WRITER

✳

Love is the delusion that one woman differs from another.

H. L. MENCKEN, JOURNALIST, CRITIC, AND EDITOR

✳

The chief reason why marriage is rarely a success is that it is contracted while the partners are insane.

JOSEPH COLLINS, WRITER

✳ ✳ ✳

Spouse: someone who'll stand by you through all the trouble you wouldn't have had if you'd stayed single.

—ANONYMOUS

✳ ✳ ✳

A woman needs a man like a fish needs a bicycle.

FEMINIST SLOGAN, 1970S

* * *

The only time a woman really succeeds in changing a man is when he is a baby.
—NATALIE WOOD, ACTRESS

* * *

A man's worst difficulties begin when he is able to do as he likes.

T. H. HUXLEY, SCIENTIST

*

The trouble with Ian [Fleming] is that he gets off with women because he can't get on with them.

ROSAMOND LEHMANN, NOVELIST

*

Marriage is a great institution, but I'm not ready for an institution.

MAE WEST, ACTRESS

*

There is no fury like an ex-wife searching for a new lover.

CYRIL CONNOLLY, WRITER AND CRITIC

*

If you catch a man, throw him back.

WOMEN'S LIB SLOGAN, 1970S

Outside every thin girl is a fat man,
trying to get in.
—Katharine Whitehorn,
journalist and writer

✳ ✳ ✳

Many a man has fallen in love with a girl in a light so dim he would not have chosen a suit by it.

Maurice Chevalier, actor

✳

My wife and I tried to breakfast together, but we had to stop or our marriage would have been wrecked.

Winston Churchill,
British prime minister

✳

A wedding is just like a funeral except that you get to smell your own flowers.

Grace Hansen, author

✳ ✳ ✳

I have nothing against women—after all, it
was a woman who drove me to drink, and
I've never written to thank her for it.
—W. C. Fields, actor and comedian

✳ ✳ ✳

Women are like elephants to me: nice to look at, but I wouldn't want to own one.

W. C. FIELDS

✳

Love matches are made by people who are content, for a month of honey, to condemn themselves to a life of vinegar.

MARGUERITE, COUNTESS OF BLESSINGTON, WRITER

✳

I bequeath all my property to my wife, on condition that she remarry immediately. Then there will be at least one man to regret my death.

HEINRICH HEINE, POET (IN HIS WILL)

I never knew what real happiness was until I got married. And by then it was too late.
—MAX KAUFFMAN, AUTHOR

✳ ✳ ✳

A woman's mind is cleaner than a man's. She changes it more often.
 OLIVER HERFORD, AUTHOR AND ILLUSTRATOR

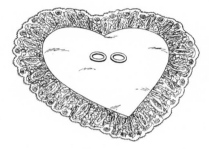

Love, n.: *a temporary insanity curable by marriage.*
Marriage, n.: *the state or condition of a community consisting of a master, a mistress and two slaves, making in all, two.*

AMBROSE BIERCE

✻

The old woman was not only ugly with the ugliness age brings us all but showed signs of formidable ugliness by birth—pickle-jar chin, mainsail ears and a nose like a trigonometry problem. What's more, she had the deep frown and snit wrinkles that come from a lifetime of bad character.

P. J. O'ROURKE, SATIRIST AND JOURNALIST

✻ ✻ ✻

Marriage is give and take. You'd better give
it to her, or she'll take it anyway.
—JOEY ADAMS, HUMORIST

✻ ✻ ✻

The one charm of marriage is that it makes a life of deception absolutely necessary for both parties.

> Oscar Wilde, playwright and poet
> (from *The Picture of Dorian Gray*)

⁎

I sometimes think that God, in creating man, somewhat overestimated His ability.

> Oscar Wilde

⁎

Rich bachelors should be heavily taxed. It is not fair that some men should be happier than others.

> Oscar Wilde

⁎

Women's intuition is the result of millions of years of not thinking.

> Rupert Hughes, author

My husband and I divorced over religious differences. He thought he was God, and I didn't.

ANONYMOUS

*

All husbands are alike, but they have different faces so you can tell them apart.

ANONYMOUS

*

Marriage is a romance in which the hero dies in the first chapter.

ANONYMOUS

* * *

You have two choices in life:
You can stay single and be miserable,
or get married and wish you were dead.
—ANONYMOUS

* * *

Rantings of a Miserable Old Bastard: Part 4

Dentists' drills: Now why, in the name of all that's humane, hasn't somebody invented a dentist's drill that doesn't go *zzzzeeeeeeeeeee, zzzzeeeeeeeeeee?* Better still, it's been reported that scientists are trying to develop ways of treating cavities without the use of drills. Well, why don't they get on with it?

DANDRUFF: Other people's, usually. And these dandruff-ridden folk are always sitting in front of you on buses, and you have to keep a beady eye on your kneecaps for any stray flakes of dandruff that fall off the shoulders of their coats and drop on you delicately. Ugh! *They* might be happy to have shoulders that look as if Mount Etna's just coughed again and flung a ton of ash all over the place, but innocent bystanders or fellow travelers are definitely not.

MAPS: Not only can you never fold the damn things back again, the place you want to be is always right in the crease of the most folded part. As for those silly things in the middle of town centers that tell you, "You are here," how do they know? You didn't tell them you were coming.

THREE THIRTY IN THE MORNING: Whenever you have one of those dark nights of the soul, this is the time you experience it—all at once.

You wake up at 3:30 in the morning, in a sweat, as, almost palpably, your self-awareness crashes into your skull as if it were downloaded from a celestial server: you recall who you are, where you are, and at what point in your life you are; you acknowledge your mortality, your debts, and your guilt at whatever it was you did last night and throughout all your life so far; you add up your failures, your low moments, and are horrified at the thought that they'll continue for the rest of your life, which you suddenly wish would end right now, if only you had put all your affairs in order, which you haven't. You do whatever you normally do to try to get back to sleep, and invariably fail. Yep, 3:30 a.m. should be banished from the clock face by international agreement.

Flies: They refuse to go away. *Bzz, bzz.* You go *swat, swat.* And they just go *bzz, bzz.* They land on your knife or the rim of your beer glass or wine glass. *Bzz, bzz.* And do you know what the disgusting creatures do once they land? They throw up, that's what they do. No manners. What they're actually doing is upchucking digestive enzymes to liquefy food. And they have 1,500 taste hairs on their feet, so they've already decided the rim of your cup or your knife is going to yield some goodies. Anyway, you decide flypaper is hideous and you don't want to spray poisons in your house so you put one of those ultraviolet fly zappers up in your kitchen, and they *bzz, bzz* to the other end of the room and make a nuisance of themselves there. Here's a secret. They have compound eyes, so they can see you coming with that rolled-up copy of *The Sunday Times.* A fly sees your movements and it's off. *Bzz, bzz.* But approach very, very slowly. They can detect movement only down to a certain speed, you see. Bang! *Bzz, splat!* You got him.

BOOM, BOOM: Only people who are totally brain-dead but generous of spirit would want you to share their music with them wherever they go—so much so that you can't even hear yourself think with the noise of the bass from their ultramega, superduper ear-shredder, extra-woofer, new ThunderSound Shatterblaster speaker system, which is using their car's own structure as an amplifier to make it more ultra, more mega, more super, more damn duper, and adding an extra dimension of wooferistic megabass banality. And they very likely have the speakers in the doors. Do these thoughtless idiots realize they run the risk of going deaf by the time they turn thirty?

CALL CENTERS: First, it's the seemingly endless menu. "You have six options." You select one. "You now have eight more options." You swear under your breath and select one. "Please select from the following five options." You swear some more, louder this time, jump up and down, then select an option. "If your mother has a maiden name, please select 1." Despair begins to darken your very soul. You hang up, take a deep breath, count to ten, and throw the phone out of the nearest open window.

BLACKBOARDS AND FINGERNAILS: No need even to explain this one. Just putting those two words within a gnat's hair of each other has got your teeth on edge and sent a shiver running down your spine.

Oh Come,
All Ye Morons,
or
'Tis the Season to Be Grouchy

"Bah," said Scrooge.
"Humbug!"

—CHARLES DICKENS
(FROM *A Christmas Carol*)

I t's that time again. Streets are turned into gaudy thoroughfares with sickly colored lights; carols and other jolly nonsense are spilling out from loudspeakers in stores; shelves are bristling with wrapping paper in festively garish colors; you can't buy what you want to buy because everything on sale is seasonal; ads on

TV show morons wearing paper hats, partying; people who don't drink at other times of the year stagger out of bars, drunk as a skunk, unable to hold their beer. Yes, it's that time again: September.

It gets earlier every year. But how long will it be before *next* Christmas starts at the end of *this* Christmas? There should be a law against it. And it's all the fault of the shops and the multi-mega-supermarkets. If it

weren't for companies' obsessions with filling your home with a load of crap, there'd be a nice, respectable eleven-month gap between this Christmas and next.

In the old days you looked forward to the special, joyous few weeks when the anticipation kicked in, then Christmas Eve arrived, followed by the day itself, then winding down with some partying on New Year's Eve to bid the season *au revoir* for another year. But in modern times, how can you enjoy it now that it's virtually all year-round? We've all been robbed of our childhood, thanks to the money-grubbing marketing men. Ebenezer Scrooge had it about right: humbug.

Though Christmas is traditionally a time for family get-togethers, sometimes you wish you'd never bothered. Tensions invariably run high, long-held grudges rear their ugly head once the demon drink starts flowing, and before you know it you've got a familial disagreement of civil war proportions on your hands. Peace and goodwill to all? Hardly.

There are other annual events that turn people into utter fools. You go down the street, and that dizzy woman three houses down has adorned the outside of her house with banners and balloons because her twit of a husband has reached his fortieth birthday and she thinks it's a really, really good idea to tell the entire street about it. Oh, terrific for him, you don't say as you think grouchily, "She's a moron for doing it, and he's a *total* moron for letting her."

Then there is the annual vacation, when all the lemmings swamp the interstates and airline departure gates, complaining about how crowded everything is and failing spectacularly to realize that *they* are the ones contributing to the problem. Idiots. Off they go to blow a year's savings on overpriced hotels and restaurants, and they come back with skin the color of boot polish and think it's an achievement that they've got a tan.

From Christmas and New Year to birthday celebrations and holidays, sometimes you're better off staying at home. But we won't go on about it, and instead offer some alternative points of view.

Quotable Querulous Quibbles about Special Occasions

Why for fifty-three years I've put up with it now! I MUST stop Christmas from coming! . . . But HOW?

Dr. Seuss, writer and illustrator
(said by the Grinch in *How the Grinch Stole Christmas*)

After all, what are birthdays? Here today and gone tomorrow.

—Eeyore (from A. A. Milne's *The House at Pooh Corner*)

✳ ✳ ✳

In England you worship two goddesses: one is Christmas, the other one is holidays. As soon as they finish advertising for Christmas on television and in the papers, the next big thing is the annual holiday.

BUCHI EMECHETA, NOVELIST AND PUBLISHER

✳

He . . . threw them about the room saying: "We always smash our Christmas presents straight away; we don't want any." Smashing his toys thus stood in his unconscious for smashing his father's genitals. During this first hour he did in fact break several toys.

MELANIE KLEIN, PSYCHOANALYST

✳ ✳ ✳

Darkness is cheap, and Scrooge liked it.
—CHARLES DICKENS, NOVELIST
(FROM *A Christmas Carol*)

✳ ✳ ✳

"Merry Christmas! Out upon merry Christmas! What's Christmas time to you but a time for paying bills without money; a time for finding yourself a year older, but not an hour richer; a time for balancing your books and having every item in 'em through a round dozen of months presented dead against you? If I could work my will," said Scrooge indignantly, "every idiot who goes about with 'Merry Christmas' on his lips, should be boiled with his own pudding, and buried with a stake of holly through his heart. He should!"

CHARLES DICKENS (FROM *A Christmas Carol*)

The Wit of Being a Miserable Old Bastard,

or

How to Be Moody and Funny at the Same Time

J ust because you spend most of your life in a state of doom and gloom, and you've barely got a good word to say about anybody or anything, it doesn't mean your negative attitude and observations shouldn't raise a few laughs at the same time.

A great many successful comedians have made a career out of being a humorous old grump (W. C. Fields and Groucho Marx, for example), so why not follow their lead? A cutting criticism or a rude riposte uttered by a cranky curmudgeon can be a source of great amusement to observers, albeit at the expense of the unfortunate subject of the remark. So to bring this miserable tome to a fitting end, read and learn from the mirth-making masters of moodiness:

Putting down politicians

I have seen better-looking faces on pirate flags.

ANONYMOUS REMARK MADE ABOUT
BRITISH PRIME MINISTER SIR ALEC DOUGLAS-HOME

It has been a political career of this man to begin with hypocrisy, proceed with arrogance, and to finish with contempt.

Thomas Paine, political writer
(on President John Adams)

✳

He is undoubtedly living proof that a pig's bladder on a stick can be elected as a member of parliament.

Tony Banks, British politician
(on fellow MP Terry Dicks)

✳ ✳ ✳

Gerry Ford is so dumb that he can't fart and chew gum at the same time.
—President Lyndon B. Johnson,
(on future President Gerald Ford)

✳ ✳ ✳

Major is what he is: a man from nowhere, going nowhere, heading for a well-merited obscurity as fast as his mediocre talents can carry him.

Paul Johnson, journalist
(on British Prime Minister John Major)

✳

Malcolm Fraser could be described as a cutlery man—he was born with a silver spoon in his mouth and he uses it to stab his colleagues in the back.

Bob Hawke, union leader and later
Australian prime minister (referring to
the then Australian prime minister)

Richard Nixon is a no-good lying bastard.
He can lie out of both sides of his mouth
at the same time, and if he ever caught
himself telling the truth he'd lie just to
keep his hand in.
—President Harry S. Truman

✳ ✳ ✳

A modest little man with much to be modest about.
Winston Churchill, British prime minister
(on his successor, Clement Attlee)

*Whenever Stafford has tried to increase the sum of human happiness,
grass never grows again.*
Anonymous remark made
about politician Sir Stafford Cripps

✳

A political leader worthy of assassination.
Irving Layton, writer (on Canadian
Prime Minister Pierre Trudeau)

Of all the men, whom it was ever my lot to accost and to waste civilities upon, Adams was the most doggedly and systematically repulsive. With a vinegar aspect, cotton in his leathern ears, and hatred of England in his heart, he sat in the frivolous assemblies of Petersburg like a bulldog among spaniels.
—W. H. Lyttelton, writer
(on President John Quincy Adams)

* * *

As an intellectual, he bestowed upon the games of golf and bridge all the enthusiasm and perseverance that he withheld from books and ideas.
Emmet John Hughes, writer
(on President Dwight D. Eisenhower)

*

The word "honor" in the mouth of Mr. Webster is like the word "love" in the mouth of a whore.

Ralph Waldo Emerson, essayist
(on politician Daniel Webster)

Government: a kind of legalized pillage.
—KIN HUBBARD, HUMORIST

✷ ✷ ✷

When they circumcised Herbert Samuel, they threw away the wrong bit.

ATTRIBUTED TO DAVID LLOYD GEORGE,
BRITISH PRIME MINISTER
(ON FELLOW POLITICIAN HERBERT SAMUEL)

✷

He sailed through American history like a steel ship loaded with mono-liths of granite.

H. L. MENCKEN, JOURNALIST AND
CRITIC (ON PRESIDENT GROVER CLEVELAND)

✷

A tin-horn politician with the manner of a rural corn doctor and the mien of a ham actor.

H. L. MENCKEN
(ON PRESIDENT WARREN G. HARDING)

✷ ✷ ✷

A good politician is as unthinkable as an honest burglar.
—H. L. MENCKEN

✷ ✷ ✷

Randolph Churchill went into the hospital . . . to have a lung removed. It was announced that the trouble was not "malignant." . . . I remarked that it was a typical triumph of modern science to find the only part of Randolph that was not malignant and remove it.

Evelyn Waugh, writer (in his diary)

His temper, naturally morose, has become licentiously peevish. Crossed in his cabinet, he insults the House of Lords and plagues the most eminent of his colleagues with the crabbed malice of a maundering witch.
—Benjamin Disraeli, British prime minister (on fellow politician the Earl of Aberdeen)

* * *

If Gladstone fell into the Thames that would be a misfortune, and if anybody pulled him out that, I suppose, would be a calamity.

Benjamin Disraeli (on British Prime Minister William Gladstone)

On players from the world of film

She turned down the role of Helen Keller because she couldn't remember the lines.

JOAN RIVERS, COMEDIAN (ON ACTRESS BO DEREK)

✳ ✳ ✳

If Greta really wants to be alone, she should come to a performance of one of her films in Dublin.

—UNKNOWN IRISH CRITIC
(ON ACTRESS GRETA GARBO)

✳ ✳ ✳

Working with her [Julie Andrews] is like being hit over the head with a Valentine's card.

CHRISTOPHER PLUMMER, ACTOR

✳

He looks as if his idea of fun would be to find a cold damp grave and sit in it.

RICHARD WINNINGTON, CRITIC
(ON ACTOR PAUL HENREID)

✳

He's the kind of guy who, if you say, "Hiya, Clark, how are you?" is stuck for an answer.

AVA GARDNER, ACTRESS
(ON FELLOW ACTOR CLARK GABLE)

She is uniquely suited to play a woman of limited intelligence.
> Harry and Michael Medved, film critics
> (on actress Farrah Fawcett)

✳

As wholesome as a bowl of cornflakes, and at least as sexy.
> Dwight Macdonald, critic
> (describing actress Doris Day)

✳

Acting is like rollerskating: once you know how to do it, it is neither stimulating nor exciting.
> George Sanders, actor

✳

A walking X-ray.
> Oscar Levant, wit (on actress Audrey Hepburn)

✳

A man of many talents—all of them minor.
> Leslie Halliwell, film historian
> (on film director Blake Edwards)

✳ ✳ ✳

Overweight, overbosomed, overpaid, and under-talented, she set the acting profession back a decade.
—David Susskind, producer and talk-show host (on actress Elizabeth Taylor)

✳ ✳ ✳

She has only two expressions—
joy and indigestion.
—Dorothy Parker, humorist, critic, and
writer (on actress Marion Davies)

✳ ✳ ✳

To me, Edith looks like something that would eat its young.
Dorothy Parker (on actress Dame Edith Evans)

✳

A vacuum with nipples.

Otto Preminger, film director
(on actress Marilyn Monroe)

✳

There are two kinds of directors in the theater: those who think they are
God, and those who are certain of it.

Rhetta Hughes, actress

✳ ✳ ✳

His features resembled a fossilized washrag.
—Alan Brien, journalist
(on actor Steve McQueen)

✳ ✳ ✳

She has the face of an exhausted gnu, the voice of an unstrung tennis
racket, and a figure of no describable shape.

John Simon, critic (on actress Angelica Huston)

An acting style that's really a nervous breakdown in slow motion.
JOHN SIMON (ON ACTRESS DIANE KEATON)

✳

Diana Rigg is built like a brick mausoleum with insufficient flying buttresses.
JOHN SIMON (ON BRITISH ACTRESS DIANA RIGG)

✳

She looks like a cross between an aardvark and an albino rat surmounted by a platinum-coated horse bun.
JOHN SIMON (ON SINGER AND ACTRESS BARBRA STREISAND)

✳

The biggest bug in the manure pile.
ELIA KAZAN, FILM PRODUCER
(ON FELLOW FILM PRODUCER HARRY COHN)

✳

Oh, excuse me. I thought you were a fellow I once knew in Pittsburgh.
GROUCHO MARX TO GRETA GARBO (AFTER SHE REMOVED HER HAT)

✳

Getting personal

A fat flabby little person with the face of a baker, the clothes of a cobbler, the size of a barrelmaker, the manners of a stocking salesman, and the dress of an innkeeper.
VICTOR DE BALABIN, WRITER
(ON NOVELIST HONORÉ DE BALZAC)

This arrogant, sour, ceremonial, pious, chauvinistic egomaniac.

ELLIOT GOULD, ACTOR (ON FELLOW
ACTOR AND COMEDIAN JERRY LEWIS)

✳

To be a moral thief, an unblushing liar, a supreme dictator, and a cruel self-satisfied monster, and attain, in the minds of millions, the status of a deity, is not only remarkable, but a dismal reflection on the human race. She had much in common with Hitler, only no mustache.

—NOËL COWARD, PLAYWRIGHT (ON THE
LEADER AND FOUNDER OF THE CHRISTIAN
SCIENCE MOVEMENT, MARY BAKER EDDY)

✳

The man was a major comedian, which is to say that he had the compassion of an icicle, the effrontery of a carnival shill, and the generosity of a pawnbroker.

S. J. PERELMAN, HUMORIST
(ON COMEDIAN GROUCHO MARX)

✳

I never forget a face, but in your case I'll be glad to make an exception.

GROUCHO MARX

I've had a perfectly wonderful evening. But this wasn't it.
—GROUCHO MARX (ON LEAVING A DINNER PARTY)

Your mother could.

DOROTHY PARKER (TO A FRIEND WHO SAID
THAT SHE WOULD NOT ATTEND ONE OF PARKER'S
PARTIES BECAUSE SHE "COULD NOT BEAR FOOLS")

✳

Pearson is an infamous liar, a revolting liar, a pusillanimous liar, a lying ass, a natural-born liar, a liar by profession, a liar of living, a liar in the daytime, a liar in the nighttime, a dishonest, ignorant, corrupt, and groveling crook.

SENATOR KENNETH MCKELLAR
(ON JOURNALIST DREW PEARSON)

Englishwomen's shoes look as if they had been made by someone who had often heard shoes described, but who had never seen any.

ANONYMOUS

✻

I do not think that I shall ever forget the sight of [Mount] Etna at sunset . . . Nothing I have ever seen in Art or Nature was quite so revolting.

EVELYN WAUGH (IN HIS DIARY)

A tub of pork and beer.
—HECTOR BERLIOZ, COMPOSER
(ON COMPOSER GEORGE FREDERICK HANDEL)

* * *

That grand imposter, that loathsome hypocrite, that detestable traitor . . . that landscape of iniquity, that sink of sin, that compendium of baseness, who now calls himself our protector.

THE COLORFUL VIEWS OF ANABAPTISTS ON
BRITISH LORD PROTECTOR OLIVER CROMWELL

A woman whose face looked as if it had been made of sugar and someone had licked it.

GEORGE BERNARD SHAW, PLAYWRIGHT AND
WRITER (ON DANCER ISADORA DUNCAN)

✳

Mr. Dalton's aspect and manner were repulsive. There was no gracefulness belonging to him. His voice was harsh and brawling, his gait stiff and awkward; his style of writing and conversation dry and almost crabbed.

HUMPHRY DAVY, CHEMIST
(ON FELLOW SCIENTIST JOHN DALTON)

On musicians and composers

The Beatles are not merely awful, I would consider it sacrilegious to say anything less than that they are god-awful. They are so unbelievably horrible, so appallingly unmusical, so dogmatically insensitive to the magic of art, that they qualify as crowned heads of anti-music.
—WILLIAM F. BUCKLEY JR.,
AUTHOR AND COMMENTATOR

✳ ✳ ✳

Mr. Jones is, in the words of his own hit, not unusual . . . at least not as a singer; as a sex symbol he is nothing short of inexplicable.

SHERIDAN MORLEY, CRITIC
(ON SINGER TOM JONES)

All legs and hair with a mouth that
could swallow the whole stadium
and the hot-dog stand.
—LAURA LEE DAVIES, MUSIC CRITIC
(ON SINGER TINA TURNER)

✳

*Listening to the Fifth Symphony of Ralph Vaughan Williams is like
staring at a cow for forty-five minutes.*

AARON COPLAND, COMPOSER
(ON FELLOW COMPOSER WILLIAMS)

*I love Wagner, but the music I prefer is that of a cat hung up by its tail
outside a window and trying to stick to the panes of glass with its claws.*
CHARLES BAUDELAIRE, POET
(ON COMPOSER RICHARD WAGNER)

✳

*Stravinsky looks like a man who was potty-trained too early, and that
music proves it as far as I'm concerned.*

RUSSELL HOBAN, WRITER
(ON COMPOSER IGOR STRAVINSKY)

Composition indeed! Decomposition is the proper word for such hated fungi, which choke up and poison the fertile plains of harmony, threatening the world with drought.

A frank review of the work
of Franz Liszt, which appeared
in *Musical World* in 1855

On dead people

The world is rid of Lord Byron, but the deadly slime of his touch still remains.

John Constable, painter
(shortly after the death of poet Byron)

✳

The reason so many people showed up at his funeral was because they wanted to make sure he was dead.

Samuel Goldwyn, film producer
(on the death of fellow producer Louis B. Mayer)

How do they know?
—Dorothy Parker
(attributed, on hearing the news that
President Calvin Coolidge was dead)

* * *

Jimmy Hoffa's most valuable contribution to the American labor movement came at the moment he stopped breathing on July 30, 1975.

DAN E. MOLDEA, JOURNALIST (ON THE UNEXPLAINED
DISAPPEARANCE OF UNION LEADER JIMMY HOFFA)

On writers and poets

Truman Capote has made lying an art. A minor art.

GORE VIDAL, WRITER

⋆

Shaw, most poisonous of all the poisonous haters of England; despiser, distorter, and denier of the plain truths whereby men live; topsy-turvy perverter of all human relationships; a menace to ordered social life; irresponsible braggart, blaring self-trumpeter; idol of opaque intellects and thwarted females; calculus of contrariwise; flipperty-gibbet Pope of chaos; portent and epitome of this generation's moral and spiritual disorder.

HENRY A. JONES, CRITIC
(ON PLAYWRIGHT AND WRITER GEORGE BERNARD SHAW)

✷ ✷ ✷

An outstandingly unpleasant man, one who cheated and stole from his friends and peed on their carpets.

—KINGSLEY AMIS, WRITER (ON POET DYLAN THOMAS)

✷ ✷ ✷

Reading Proust is like bathing in someone else's dirty water.

ALEXANDER WOOLLCOTT, WRITER
(ON NOVELIST MARCEL PROUST)

I had thought that there could be only two worse writers than Stephen Crane, namely two Stephen Cranes.

AMBROSE BIERCE, WRITER

✻

His mind is so vile a mind, so cozy, hypocritical, praise-mad, canting, envious, concupiscent.

SAMUEL TAYLOR COLERIDGE,
POET, CRITIC, AND PHILOSOPHER
(ON NOVELIST SAMUEL RICHARDSON)

✻ ✻ ✻

A sycophant, a flatterer, a breaker of marriage vows, a whining and inconstant person.
—ELIZABETH FORSYTH, WRITER
(ON PLAYWRIGHT WILLIAM SHAKESPEARE)

Henry James has a mind so fine that no idea could violate it.

T. S. ELIOT, POET (ON NOVELIST JAMES)

There are two ways of disliking poetry: one way is to dislike it, the other is to read Pope.

OSCAR WILDE, PLAYWRIGHT AND POET (ON POET ALEXANDER POPE)

✻

As a writer he mastered everything except language, as a novelist he can do everything except tell a story, as an artist everything except articulate.

OSCAR WILDE (ON NOVELIST GEORGE MEREDITH)

✻

Shaw is the most fraudulent, inept writer of Victorian melodrama ever to gull a timid critic or fool a dull public.

JOHN OSBORNE, PLAYWRIGHT
(ON PLAYWRIGHT AND WRITER GEORGE BERNARD SHAW)

✳ ✳ ✳

On the Road—that's not writing,
that's typing.
—TRUMAN CAPOTE, WRITER (ON NOVELIST
JACK KEROUAC'S BEST-KNOWN WORK)

✳ ✳ ✳

A disgusting common little man. He had never been taught how to avoid being offensive.

DAME REBECCA WEST, NOVELIST
(ON WRITER EVELYN WAUGH)

Longfellow is to poetry what the barrel organ is to music.
—VAN WYCK BROOKS, CRITIC
(ON POET HENRY WADSWORTH LONGFELLOW)

✳ ✳ ✳

So boring, you fall asleep halfway through her name.

ALAN BENNETT, WRITER
(ON WRITER ARIANNA STASSINOPOULOS)

✳

The first 200 pages of Ulysses—*never have I read such tosh. As for the first two chapters we will let them pass, but the third, fourth, fifth, sixth—merely the scratchings of pimples on the body of the bootboy at Claridge's.*

VIRGINIA WOOLF, NOVELIST
(ON WRITER JAMES JOYCE'S NOVEL *Ulysses*)

He is limp and damp and milder than the breath of a cow.
—VIRGINIA WOOLF
(ON FELLOW WRITER E. M. FORSTER)

✳ ✳ ✳

Shelley should not be read, but inhaled through a gas pipe.
LIONEL TRILLING, CRITIC (ON POET PERCY BYSSHE SHELLEY)

✳

Thomas Gray walks as if he had fouled his small-clothes and looks as if he smelt it.
CHRISTOPHER SMART, POET (ON FELLOW POET GRAY)

✳

Gibbon is an ugly, affected, disgusting fellow, and poisons our literary club for me. I class him among infidel wasps and venomous insects.
JAMES BOSWELL, WRITER AND BIOGRAPHER
(ON HISTORIAN EDWARD GIBBON, AUTHOR OF
The History of the Decline and Fall of the Roman Empire)

On monarchs

A pig, an ass, a dunghill, the spawn of an adder, a basilisk, a lying buffoon, a mad fool with a frothy mouth.
MARTIN LUTHER, PROTESTANT THEOLOGIAN
AND REFORMER (ON KING HENRY VIII)

His intellect is of no more use than a pistol packed in the bottom of a trunk if one were attacked in the robber-infested Apennines.
PRINCE ALBERT (ON HIS SON THE
PRINCE OF WALES, LATER EDWARD VII)

⁂

As just and merciful as Nero, and as good a Christian as Mahomet.
JOHN WESLEY, PREACHER (ON QUEEN ELIZABETH I)

Nowadays, a parlor maid as ignorant
as Queen Victoria was when she
came to the throne would be classed
as mentally defective.
—GEORGE BERNARD SHAW

✳ ✳ ✳

A more contemptible, cowardly, selfish, unfeeling dog does not exist than this king . . . with vices and weaknesses of the lowest and most contemptible order.
CHARLES GREVILLE, DIARIST (ON KING GEORGE IV)

On artists

A decorator tainted with insanity.
        Kenyon Cox, critic (on painter Paul Gauguin)

✳ ✳ ✳

The last bit of methane left in the intestine of the dead cow that is postmodernism.
—Robert Hughes, art critic (on artist Jeff Koons)

✳ ✳ ✳

He bores me. He ought to have stuck to his flying machines.
        Auguste Renoir, painter (on artist Leonardo da Vinci)

Trading punches

Nancy Astor: *Winston, if I were your wife I would put poison in your coffee.*

Winston Churchill: *Nancy, if I were your husband I would drink it.*

✴

Earl of Sandwich: *'Pon my soul, Wilkes, I don't know whether you'll die upon the gallows or of the pox.*

John Wilkes: *That depends, my Lord, whether I first embrace your Lordship's principles, or your Lordship's mistresses.*

THE MARQUESS OF LONDONDERRY: *Have you read my last book, Winston?*

WINSTON CHURCHILL: *No, I only read for pleasure or for profit.*

✳

GEORGE BERNARD SHAW *(in a letter to Winston Churchill inviting him to the first night of his new play* St. Joan*): Bring a friend—if you have one.*

WINSTON CHURCHILL *(in his reply): I cannot come. Would it be possible for you to let me have tickets for the second night—if there is one.*

✳

PAMELA HARRIMAN *(the socialite and diplomat, ushering Dorothy Parker into a party ahead of her): Age before beauty.*

DOROTHY PARKER: *Pearls before swine.*

Last word

I'm free of all prejudices. I hate everyone equally.
—W. C. FIELDS, ACTOR AND COMEDIAN